"Like all epic road trips, Shawn &
interior mileage, from one state of ı
blue bus does the physical miles ac
book is many things: a travelogue, a parenting manual, a spiritual
narrative. But most of all, it's an engrossing tale told by two wise
and thoughtful writers. Don't read it if you're not prepared for the
oncoming wanderlust."

- **Jason Boyett**, author of *O Me of Little Faith*
and *Pocket Guide to the Afterlife*

"This is a grand little tale of trundling about the country with
Shawn and Maile and their family in a big old bus named Willie.
But it's also about something so much deeper, a journey within a
journey. It's about the risks involved in taking a road few dare to
travel. It's about adventure and searching, about finding the
beautiful and the good, as well as the bad and the ugly. And it's all
written from a heart that unflinchingly faces and tells of the
suffering of those abandoned and lonely souls scattered along life's
highway."

- **Ira Wagler,** author of New York Times Bestseller,
Growing Up Amish

"We all have lists of things we want to do someday when life slows
down or when the kids grow up or when we have more money.
Shawn and Maile show us what it's like to drop everything and live
the adventure of a lifetime. They don't pull any punches, and like
any good adventure story, theirs helps you to see that it wasn't the
destination that mattered, but the journey."

- **Darrell Vesterfelt**, President, *Prodigal Magazine*

How to Use a Runaway Truck Ramp

And Other Tales From

Our 10,000 Mile Adventure

To Our Parents

For Supporting Every Adventure

We've Ever Taken

This book occasionally alternates between my perspective and my wife Maile's perspective. If a section is written by Maile, you'll see her name at the beginning like this:

Maile

Also, if the section is one of Maile's blog posts, it will be in italics.

Otherwise, you can assume you're reading my words.

June, 2012
(or one week after The Trip)

After we returned from The Trip, strange dreams plagued my sleep, visions of scowling grizzly bears and highways that never ended and mountains that rose up in front of me, white and foaming like tidal waves. I dreamed of being trapped in tight spaces. I dreamed of careening over a mountainside, the bus's brakes failing. We crashed through a guardrail, plummeted thousands of feet, and just as the bus was about to make impact with the tops of the trees, I gasped and woke up.

I was alive. We had survived.

A local television anchorman came to the house to interview us during those glazed-over days just after we had returned from The Trip. This particular anchorman had seen us off, four months before, with an interview that aired on the local news, and he had asked me to let him know when we made it home.

1

The news truck pulled into my parents' driveway, and when he came to the door, we shook hands and smiled and felt like old friends. He was as fascinated as ever by our epic journey. First, he interviewed Maile, and she answered his questions with grace and that beautiful smile. Then, I sat down in the chair. The cameraman fished the microphone wire up through my shirt. I squirmed.

The anchorman asked me question after question, and I settled into a groove of answers, the words coming easily. Thinking back over that trip, from which we had so recently returned (relatively unscathed) was fun. Then something uncomfortable happened: he asked me a question I wasn't sure how to answer.

"So how do you think this trip has changed you?" he asked.

I didn't know what to say. I felt changed. I felt very changed. I thought through our experiences during those four months on the road. Every emotion, from boredom to terror, excitement to annoyance, freedom to entrapment. My mind wandered back through the glorious structure that trip had become, and I realized I couldn't articulate how I had changed because I couldn't find my old self. Somewhere along the road, my old self had been lost, and this was what remained. This new me.

I blurted out some kind of an answer to his question, but for the next few days, I found myself revisiting it. *How had I changed?* I thought back through our adventure of a lifetime, and I tried to figure out when the old me had disembarked from the bus without getting back on.

Adventures will change you. They'll saturate you with a fresh view of life. They'll take every foundation you ever stood on and shake them until they crack. Adventures will tear away layer after layer of you, and in the end, when it's all over, you'll step away from that pile of old skins and barely recognize the person you have become.

This is the story of our transformation.

The girls: Maile, Lucy and Abra.

September, 2011

(or five months before The Trip)

"Dreams, if they're any good, are always a little bit crazy." - Ray Charles

Maile

"Babe, check out this one!" Shawn called to me from the thin metal steps leading into the taupe, cushioned interior of a new RV parked inside the Great Frederick Fairgrounds in Maryland. Every year, we worked at the fair with Shawn's parents at their Pennsylvania Dutch Foods stand, and every year we toured the small collection of RVs a local dealer displayed for road trip junkies like us.

"Wow," I murmured as my eyes took in the stylishly economic kitchen and cozy bunks. In a far off corner of my mind, I had a

5

dreamy picture of my four little babes snuggled in the corners of those bunks reading books while Shawn and I sat at the vinyl booth planning the next stop on our cross-country road trip. But it was just that: a dream. And every year we talked and laughed about the possibility of it actually happening, of driving through deserts, of standing on the edges of grand canyons, of tapping our toes in an unfamiliar ocean, of seeing animals that only existed in books. But the possibility of it happening, really happening, seemed, at best, remote.

For at least a decade, we dreamed about it, made mental lists of the sights we'd see or the restaurants we'd eat at or the friends we'd visit. At one point, before the stork started arriving with babies, Shawn and I joked that we'd take to the road in a semi, make our living as truck drivers and simultaneously soaking in the country.

But the adventure eluded us. Life got bogged down in school routines and paying the mortgage and changing diapers. We imagined that adventure wasn't for this immediate stage of life; we'd pacify ourselves by saying, "maybe when the kids are older," or "once we're retired, we'll do it." Still, it seemed such a pity to have an exciting dream with a departure date decades away.

If ever at all.

Then in the summer of 2009, our life took an unexpected turn. Shawn's painting business in Virginia was bleeding money (as was our personal bank account), and the only way to stop it was to close up shop, leave the house and friends we loved, and move into my in-laws' basement in Pennsylvania to start from scratch, all over again. But this time we made a commitment to ourselves and to God: we weren't going back down the same old road we had covered time and again in our decade of marriage: we were tired of living a mediocre life today, sacrificing our passions and dreams, in hopes that we'd get to do what we really wanted someday far off in the distance. We decided to stay true to the passions God put in our hearts, no matter where that led us.

For two years, we did just that. Ever since college, Shawn had wanted to make a living writing. So when we left Virginia, he began spending his days (and nights) co-writing books and blogging while I homeschooled the kids. We survived on a fairly meager income while renting a cozy little double-wide trailer on 3 acres in a wooded valley and paying down the debt our failed business had accumulated. And like daffodils in the first warm rays of the springtime sun, our dreams started to blossom.

In the fall of 2011, we decided to up the departure date for our cross-country trip by a couple of decades. Circumstances fell into place with providential ease, and by the middle of December, we began packing up our double-wide and making plans for traveling the U.S. for four months with our four young children in a big blue bus we would affectionately call "Willie." And if the level of "crazy" determines the worth of a dream, we would soon discover that ours was pure gold.

The boys: Cade, Shawn and Sam (aka Sammy, "Red Rackham," and Samuel James when it's been a long day).

January 2012

(or one month before the trip)

"I am looking for someone to share in an adventure that I am arranging, and it's very difficult to find anyone."

"I should think so — in these parts! We are plain quiet folk and have no use for adventures. Nasty disturbing uncomfortable things! Make you late for dinner!"

J.R.R. Tolkien,

Maile didn't wake up when I pushed back the covers and gently eased my way out of the bed. I crept through the house that night, through the dark. Outside, it was January, and cold. The heater kicked on every few minutes, forcing air through the vents in the floor.

I walked to the opposite side of the house and peeked in to the girls' room where seven-year-old Lucy shared a bed with three-year-old Abra. Seeing their small, sleeping faces in the meager light was like catching a glimpse into some other world: a fairytale, perhaps, where two little girls have fallen into a deep sleep from which they cannot wake. I couldn't resist – I kissed them both on the forehead, then walked to the neighboring room.

Our two sons slept there: eight-year-old Cade and two-year-old Sam. Sam had rolled off of his bed onto the floor. Cade's long limbs stretched from one side of the small bed to the other. It was like looking at two separate versions of myself from the past, two carbon copies yanked from photo albums of my childhood and made real, here, in this house.

I walked back out to the living room and sat there in the dark. In that middle-of-the-night moment, the idea of our impending grand adventure overwhelmed me: driving 10,000 miles around the country in my uncle's 40' bus (all while towing our minivan along behind) felt as far from the realm of possibility as going to the moon. I closed my eyes for a moment and tried to picture it, what it would be like, but I didn't see it. I couldn't see it.

And that's probably a good thing: I didn't see the ignition falling into the dash or the bus overheating in Arizona and Nevada. I didn't see the problems with the waste tank or the ever-rising gas prices devouring our tiny savings account. I didn't see our family of six perched high on a west coast hill, wrapped in a sleeping bag, watching the sun set. I didn't see the view from the top of the Teton Pass at 8,000 feet, or how our brakes would go out on that 10% downhill grade.

10

I simply went to bed with a to-do list in my mind, and eventually, I fell back to sleep.

Yet, no sooner had we begun preparing for our trip than the real feeling of adventure descended around us. Because no matter how exciting an adventure may sound during its conception, as soon as preparation begins in earnest, you realize why people are so in love with the idea of adventures and yet so rarely embark upon them.

Suddenly, we spent every waking hour packing. And planning. And buying cheap cereal at BB's, our local discount grocery. Our house became a disaster zone. Piles formed: the "bus pile," the "thrift store" pile, the "storage unit" pile, the "I-have-no-idea-what-this-is-or-what-we-should-do-with-it" pile. We lived in a half-packed house for weeks. We felt like nomads and began to doubt our resolve.

Then, on the day we needed to move the last of our things into storage, it snowed. It took me an hour to clean off the cars and get them up the driveway. When I think back to that morning, I hear the sound of tires spinning in the muffled silence of a snowy day. I see four kids grapple with the idea of leaving the house we loved.

With the help of some dear friends, we moved our things on that snowy day. With the help of some other dear friends later that night, we celebrated our impending departure with raised wine glasses. We basked in the presence of their adoration over our bravery and our sure success.

But perhaps the thing that nagged me the most during those weeks of preparation for our adventure was an unexpected emotion creeping in around the edges of my mind. Something I hesitate to admit. Something I felt during that late-night walk through the house on a January night, weeks before we were scheduled to leave.

I was afraid.

What if I wreck the bus? What if we run out of money on the trip? What if my writing business dries up while I'm on the road? What if we have to move back in with our parents?

Interesting. All of those worries would come true. But there were more:

What if we come back to Lancaster unchanged? What if we come back totally different people? What if we never come back?

What if the price of diesel goes up to $7.00 a gallon? What if the bus breaks down in the middle of Wyoming? What if, after three weeks, we hate it on the bus? What if, after four months, we love it so much we never want to live in a normal house again?

But as I thought through those fears, both the rational and the irrational, I began to understand something: fear is an ever-present companion on any great adventure. For better or for worse, what makes an adventure adventurous is the presence of this uncertainty, this trepidation, this fear.

12

I could run from fear and turn down the adventure. I could run from fear and continue to live a life when I'm never late for dinner. Or I could stare at my fear, move in towards it, and eventually pass through it.

So there I was, afraid. But fear would not stop us.

"It's time to move on, time to get going
What lies ahead, I have no way of knowing
But under my feet, baby, grass is growing
It's time to move on, it's time to get going."

Tom Petty

Then, it was finished.

The house we had lived in for the previous two years sat empty at the bottom of the hill. The chicken coop that my dad and I had built out of two old tables, some 2x4s, and chicken wire sat in the back yard, vacant. The first successful garden we had ever planted watched us drive away, then rolled over and covered itself in winter brown and a tangled mess of still-present autumn weeds, dead and lined with traces of snow.

There was a flat stretch of yard between the house and the garden – as we had finished packing up, I went out and removed the small stakes used to mark soccer goals. There were many 10-9 games on that pitch that will go down in the record books. The inadvertent

14

goal off of Abra's head came to mind – it was a shot that had all of us falling to our knees in laughter (all of us except Abra – she stood there with a smile on her face, confused, thinking she had done something rather wonderful – which, of course, she had).

The World Cup had nothing on us.

As we drove away from that house, I thought about how the next people to live there would have no idea what some of those random things were: the small mounds of rock, like altars, where Lucy and Abra pretended to be chefs and made feasts out of pebbles; the not-quite-natural crisscrossing of fallen branches in the woods that made up our fort; the tiniest of pencil strokes on the trim in the girls room that marked their height, creeping up the door as those two years had passed. There was a tiny toy car under the woodpile, and a deflated ball up in the tree: remnants left by Cade and Sam.

Two of the hardest years of my life. We had arrived broke and broken, with only the tiniest sliver of hope remaining, like those first shoots of green in the spring. I had written up in the workshop until my pinkies were numb from the cold, and all the while, the space heater at my feet felt like the surface of the sun. I had mowed the grass, back and forth, back and forth, the previous 30-some years of my life running over and over through my mind like a bad movie I couldn't quite forget.

But they were also two of the best years of my life. It sounds rather cliché, but somehow, I found myself there in that tiny house. I found a me that I liked, a me with fingernails dirty from the garden, shoes stained green from mowing the grass. I found my family again. I found Maile again. It was a strange thing, finding so many things I had never known were lost.

But it was time, you know? It was just time to move on.

It was time to get going.

"Look, when do the really interesting things happen? Not when you've brushed your teeth and put on your pyjamas and are cozy in bed. They happen when you are cold and uncomfortable and hungry and don't have a roof over your head for the night."

Ellen Potter, *The Kneebone Boy*

When my uncle arrived at my parents' house late that night in February with the bus, the kids screamed in joyous rapture while Maile and I grinned nervously at each other before following them out the side door. We fumbled through our existing tiredness for our shoes and formed a small traffic jam just inside the door. The kids pushed and pulled, and soon, all of us fell out into the cold night air. My breath billowed in small clouds.

The bus was huge. Red and yellow lights glowed in the darkness, and my uncle emerged, grinning. He showed me all the things I needed to know about the vehicle: where to fill up with diesel, where to empty the waste tank, where to turn on the hot water heater, where to hook up the fresh water, how to prime the water pump, how to turn on all the lights, which switches controlled which functions, where to check the oil and anti-freeze, where the breaker boxes were located, how to connect to shore power, how to turn on the generator from inside the bus and, when that failed, how to manually turn it on. He pointed out all the gauges for gas, water temperature, oil pressure, and brake pressure.

Maile watched me inhale all of this information, and when I stole glances at her she looked rather skeptical – in other words, exactly how I felt. I took notes and did a lot of nodding, but by the end of my initiation, I was completely overwhelmed.

"And that's pretty much it," my uncle said. My mom drove him home, and my dad went into the house. Maile put the kids to bed in the basement bedroom of my parents' house. I wandered around inside the bus, trying to figure out why the power still wouldn't turn on or why the generator would only sputter but not roar to life. I wondered what we had gotten ourselves into.

I walked through the dark bus with a flashlight. I eyed up the kids' bunks, the tiny kitchen and even smaller bathroom. I wandered to the back and peered into the bedroom where we would spend the next four months. I sat down at the edge of the bed and sighed.

This was supposed to be the trip of a lifetime – so why couldn't I get any relief from the anxiety I was feeling?

Willie sitting in the parking lot of my parents' driveway. Yes, that is a washer in the bottom. No, we never used it.

> "No man ever steps in the same river twice, for it's not the same river and he's not the same man."

> **Heraclitus**

Starting the bus required a certain rhythm, a particular order of events. First, I turned the key in its wobbly ignition until it clicked. Sometimes, if the bus had been parked for more than a day or two, buzzers immediately sounded as the brakes replenished their air pressure. It was impossible to turn the bus on until the brake pressure reached a certain point.

Then, I pushed the red ignition button, and hopefully, the engine roared to life. Usually the bus belched a large cloud of black smoke, evidence of some small yet persistent oil leak. Once the bus was on, I pushed the small stick to the left of the seat to the D position, pressed the brake down, and pushed in the parking brake until it released with a hissing whoosh. Then, ease off the brake and the beast was in motion.

Friends came by to wish us well. They toured the bus, the spark of adventure in their own eyes, and I wanted to take all of them with us. I wanted it to be a group effort, a mass of families heading west to start a new community in an unknown frontier. But eventually, they all said good-bye, and gave us hugs, and drove back to their own lives.

I remember the moment we pulled away. My mom and some of my nephews and nieces lingered in the front yard. My kids waved to them from the windows at the front of the bus, then ran back to our bedroom and waved to them from there, until they could not go back any further and the good-byes were complete. Then they settled into the booth at the dining room table, and Maile sat on the sofa, and the rush of cold air through the small window beside me gave us the first sense that we were doing it. We were really doing it.

My dad followed behind us on his Harley Davidson for a few miles. But eventually we veered to the right, on to the highway, and he turned for home. It was one of the most wide-eyed experiences of my entire life, steering that huge bus with Maile beside me, the whole wide world visible through the oversized windows.

And that was it: the beginning. It felt much less monumental than I had expected. In fact, it felt alarmingly normal, that road spinning beneath us. Almost as if it had been waiting.

> "It is good to have an end to journey toward; but it is the journey that matters, in the end."
>
> **Ernest Hemingway**

The generator hummed under the bus, like the constant snoring of a contented man. The small spotlights shone down on me, and on the kids, and on their endless chatter. They were a host of sparrows on a warmer-than-usual spring morning, except it was dark out, and cold.

All four of them sat at the tiny dining room table with a huge plastic container of crayons in front of them. They spilled rainbows onto their pages, unaware of the magic.

The drive from my parents' house in Paradise, PA to Gettysburg, PA, a mere hour and a half away, had been fraught with danger, seeing as that was the first long stretch that I had driven. But all went according to plan. Except for the second roundabout close to New Oxford, when the long sweeping turn threw open the refrigerator and it vomited its contents on to the floor. So long water filter, now nothing more than splintered plastic in the trash. Sort of like our past life.

That night a young couple knocked on our bus door. They were the first of the "creatives" we hoped to meet on this journey. All throughout the United States, we had many cyber-friends: bloggers and authors and poets and artists. Musicians and thespians. We planned to meet many of them for the first time in real life, putting flesh to Twitter handles and Facebook pages. It was a grand experiment in Incarnation.

Smiling, the girl handed me a paper bag, a "bus-warming" present. Travel puzzles for the kids, some trail mix, a little electronic game: they were the kinds of things a family of six can appreciate.

She was a writer and actor – her husband a musician and songwriter. We spent the evening eating bread, cheese, fruit, and (lest I be accused of being a healthy eater) some of the candy I had smuggled on to the trip. We talked about writing and creativity and the process that beckons us into the presence of those coy little creatures. When they left us a few hours later, walking down and out of the bus, I felt strangely invigorated.

"It's like we're back in college," Maile said.

"True," I replied. "Including the huge pile of laundry back in our room that needs to be put away."

Soon our four kids (the two littles and the two bigs) would be enveloped in their bunks, curtains drawn, drifting off to the sound of the rumbling generator. In a few hours, the sun would rise over Gettysburg, all those costly fields. And the sun would rise over our bus.

And our first day on the road would be behind us.

"Not I, nor anyone else can travel that road for you.
You must travel it by yourself.
It is not far. It is within reach.
Perhaps you have been on it since you were born, and did not know."

Walt Whitman

At the end of that first day I received the following email from my dad.

Hey Shawn and family,

I left you guys with mixed emotions today. Excited for you and a bit anxious and jealous all at the same time. I wanted to follow you much longer and further but knew I had to turn around at some point. It kind of felt like when you went off to college and I had to let go of you. Felt a little scary but necessary.

At Rockvale I turned around and said another prayer for you and shed more tears as I watched "Willie" crest the hill, fade into the distance, and get completely swallowed up in traffic. It didn't seem fair that no one else on the road knew what was happening in that moment.

I wanted to tell every one around you guys to be a little careful because you're not experienced yet with Willie but then I was reminded that you're a fine and capable young man now and God is with you.

So, I let you go again.

I am so proud of you and Maile in so many ways. You're the best!!! Love ya lots. Be careful and don't ever hesitate calling if you need something.

Your jealous and proud Dad

This small golden tag just behind the steering wheel reads:
"This Dog Will Hunt." Just a small relic left from the days
when Willie Nelson owned this bus.

"The purpose of life is to live it, to taste experience to the utmost, to reach out eagerly and without fear for newer and richer experience."

Eleanor Roosevelt

Maile

About a month or so before we left on our trip, Shawn and I sat down and loosely outlined the stops we wanted to make. Immediately, I began pursuing the details, lining up places to park the bus, compiling phone numbers for campgrounds, and attempting to hammer down firm dates for our arrivals and departures around the country.

"Babe, don't worry about it," Shawn said one night as I fretted over the computer, eyes scanning endless lists of state parks in California, all of which didn't allow RV's over 25 feet. "It's all gonna work out."

"Fine!" I huffed. "Fine! I just won't worry about it." I slumped back on the couch and folded my arms across my chest like a stubborn 5 year old.

And while it miffed me at the moment, that was just the advice I needed. Because whether it was out of spite or because I really recognized the wisdom in Shawn's advice, as soon as I let go of scheduling every minute of every day of every month we would be on the road, I felt lighter. Our brief stay in Gettysburg quickly taught me that the beauty in this trip wouldn't evolve from a tightly knitted schedule, but from appreciating what each location had to offer and learning the art of improvisation in the midst of it, truths I wrote about on my blog.

Cold and rainy weather welcomed us this morning. While I continued to tidy our bedroom, emptying laundry baskets stacked high with clean clothes yet to be stowed, homeschooling books, and the occasional rogue Lego, our children sprawled themselves throughout the bus, coloring, reading, and scaling the wooden trim of our desk with tiny matchbox cars.

Eventually, I got everyone dressed, five sets of teeth brushed (all the while rationing the water as I am ever watchful of filling the bus's waste tank), and myself somewhat presentable so the older two kids and I could begin our unit on the Civil War with a field trip to the Gettysburg National Military Park Museum.

On our 15-minute trek from the bus to the museum, each of the kids took a turn reading out-loud about the Civil War as I drove. "The Civil War" was a phrase they knew well, but the details remained obscure.

This last minute cram session was purely to save face. I imagined us strolling through the museum, gazing at the sepia photographs of mounted cavalrymen, when one of my children would inexplicably shout, "They rode horses in the Civil War?! Why didn't they just drive cars?! I thought this whole thing happened just a couple years ago!" Gasping museum attendants would fall faint upon the tiled floor while other visitors would whisper behind their hands, "Why doesn't that woman put her children in school? What a disgrace..."

I (and my children) would be prepared.

After we arrived at the museum, I took a few moments in the car to solidify some concepts with the kids. Once comfortable with the basics of the war, Cade confidently announced, "I would definitely be on the Union army."

"That's good to hear," I responded with a smile.

"But I'd stay in the back lines so I wouldn't get killed."

Spoken like a true child of mine. I remember studying the various wars throughout my school age years and always thinking, "I'd just flop down like a dead fish at the first opportunity and lay completely still until the coast was clear. Then, I'd crawl to safety." My son carries on my legacy.

Being a homeschooling mom, I've been to my fair share of museums, but this one was perhaps my favorite thus far. From the documentary you view before entering the museum, to the huge cyclorama of the battle, to the museum itself, I felt myself both visually and emotionally struck at every stage.

As I walked past the exhibits of the military surgeons' crude instruments or the wall collage displaying pictures of the lives lost and maimed during the battle, I felt that all my education as a child was wasted on my naïveté. I saw my younger self in my 7-year old daughter and 8-year old son, as they stood in awe by the huge horse mannequin in the cavalry exhibit or shouted, "Check this out!" after spotting the massive display of 19th century guns. In contrast, the pictures of live men now dead earned an unimpressed, "Wow," in response, and then they turned to more interesting displays.

But I, as a daughter, a sister, a wife, and a mother, stood staring at the massive wall, imagining the lives of the brothers, husbands, sons, and fathers that stared back at me through black and white. Someone mourned over the loss of these men. They gave what Lincoln called "the last full measure of devotion." They didn't lay limp on the battlefield till the enemy dispersed, then dash for the forest; they fought and died.

I certainly don't mean to judge my kids too harshly. Their innocent minds can't comprehend the sacrifices that are made to defend noble ideas like freedom and equality. I couldn't understand it till now. And perhaps that is why I love homeschooling; it reintroduces me to greatness when I have the ability to grasp it.

This first stop in Gettysburg was actually one of the last additions to our trip agenda. Knowing I had written "a trip to Gettysburg" on my objectives for this school year, I figured we should probably check it off the list before we embarked on the real "meat" of our journey. But I am so thankful for this pit stop, especially on the cusp of a cross-country excursion celebrating and appreciating the United States of America. It makes our adventure all the more meaningful.

About one week before we left for our trip, Brad Kane was interviewing us for his article in the Patriot News, *and he asked, "Aren't you afraid you'll just drive each other crazy? I mean, that's a tight space to be with 5 other people for 4 months." Of course, I went into some long-winded response about how we love spending time together and are used to tight living quarters; our current home was only about 1000 square feet, a modest space for a family of six. I droned on about how homeschooling and Shawn's "work from home" schedule were perfect preparation for a trip such as this.*

And then came the second day of our journey. After our jaunt to the Gettysburg Museum that morning, we were back by 2pm. I had the rest of the afternoon and evening before me...in rather tight quarters...with 4 rambunctious kids. I knew Shawn would be leaving at 6 pm for his writers' get-together, leaving me alone with the restless rabble.

Around 5 o'clock, I started to lose it. Sitting on the small couch in our "living room" with the two youngest taking turns scaling my back and perching on my shoulders, my body tensed with anxiety while my mind spiraled into depression:

"What on earth have I gotten myself into? I believe I signed up for the adventure with children cuddling in the corners of their bunks reading books while I sat contentedly on the couch tapping my computer's keyboard in a writer's euphoria. I want a refund."

For some odd reason, I hadn't mentally prepared myself for days cooped up with a screaming 2-year old, a whiny 3-year old, and bickering 7-and 8-year olds. This was my experience day after day at home in Pennsylvania. But there is something about "doing what you always dreamed of" that candy-coats everything. Talk about rose-colored glasses…but then your youngest son elbows you in the face during a tantrum, knocking those lenses clean off your face, putting you face-to-face with reality: nothing, not even your dream coming true, is perfect.

So when reality hit me, I staggered to the back of the bus, flopped down on our disheveled bed, and spent 10 minutes feeling sorry for myself. Then, I dressed the entire crew, herded them out to the van in the blowing rain, and drove to McDonald's.

I hate McDonald's. The food is cheap and the quality even cheaper. It's everything about food that I despise.

But I love McDonald's indoor play land. Yes, it is a disease-festering, bacteria-laden nightmare to all us mothers; but to my children, it's heaven on earth. And truthfully, to this tired mama with a serious case of cabin fever, it was a gift from God. For two sweet hours, my kids ran their little hearts out, climbing those bright blue and red tubes like a hoard of spider monkeys. And I sat cozy at a corner table tapping the keyboard in a writer's euphoria…at last.

"You know you are truly alive when you're living among lions."

Karen Blixen

I stood on the narrow road, leaning against my minivan. A layer of grit covered the hood though Maile, the kids, and I had only traveled a few hundred miles. It was Friday, three days into our four-month trip, an unseasonably warm day with a cool breeze and a bright sun. We had driven from Gettysburg, south on Route 15, and edged towards Leesburg, Virginia. The blueness of the sky seeped down through the trees, and that February day felt more like May.

But all that I felt was discouragement and disgust and anger. In front of me, twenty yards up the road, our bus was stuck.

Thirty minutes before that, I had driven down a country road somewhere around Waterford, Virginia. An endless series of horse farms sprawled out over rolling hills. But the further we went, the more stressed out I got. Those were exactly the kinds of roads I had hoped to avoid: barely paved, one and a half lanes wide, shoulderless, and lined with banks.

Then, we arrived at the lane to our friends' house: a narrow stone driveway bordered by trees. I had a very bad feeling. But I crept the bus forward.

In my first attempt, I came in a little shallow, so I backed up a few feet and tried to swing in again. Everything in my mind said stop, but I didn't want to think about it. I just wanted to do it. I wanted to park the bus and get settled for a few days and let the stress of driving untangle a bit. I tried to back up again. The bus wasn't moving. I checked my mirrors, noticing for the first time the small drainage ditch to the right of the driveway. My rear right wheels were spinning.

It's hard to explain the rage and frustration that rose up in my mind. I'm not one who usually experiences much anger. I'm generally a mellow sort of guy. But I was mad, the curtain kind of mad that clouds your brain and numbs control. I stormed out of the bus and surveyed the situation. There was no way I was getting out of that ditch on my own.

At some point during the next ten minutes, I basically kicked Maile and the kids out of the bus and told them to go to our friends' house up the lane. I made sure she knew, in no uncertain terms, that I did not want to see anyone. Not another human being. Then

I called AAA, hoping they would come and rescue us. One of our brighter moves before the trip had been to purchase a AAA policy specifically for RVs.

But when I reached one of their operators, she noted that we had just enrolled a few days before and it wouldn't take affect for 7 days. She called it an extraction and said it would not be covered. Extraction. That's exactly what it felt like. They forwarded me to a local towing company. The guy said he'd be there in 45 minutes – he had to go back and get the big truck.

I sat in the bus, waiting for the tow truck, cursing my luck over and over again. Then, in the midst of my temper tantrum, I felt a prodding inside of me.

Get out of the bus. Breathe in some fresh air. Meditate.

I was so mad I didn't want to listen, so for a few minutes, I stayed in the driver's seat, staring up the road, willing that tow truck to appear. But the Idea wouldn't let up – it didn't get louder, but it also didn't stop.

Get out of the bus. Breathe in some fresh air. Meditate.

Finally, I listened. I stumbled out of the leaning bus and walked through the soft grass to where my van sat on the shoulder of the road. I stared at Willie, leaning into the ditch, and for a moment rage threatened to consume me again. But then, I stopped. I looked

36

up at the sky, at the blue dripping through the trees, at the spring clouds somehow lost and floating through a February day.

And I waited peacefully. I took some deep breaths. I closed my eyes.

Maile made her way hesitantly out the lane. I guess she decided to risk it. She walked over to where I leaned against the van and sat on the bumper beside me.

"You know," she said quietly. "That's the thing about adventures. The stuff that happens isn't always easy. It's not always fun. But it's always worth telling."

I looked at her and nodded slowly – how could I have missed that? She was right, of course. Adventures are only adventures when it's possible for things to go horribly wrong. I thought of the Tolkien quote my friend Dave had put on my Facebook page not too many days before that:

"It's a dangerous business, Frodo, going out your door. You step onto the road, and if you don't keep your feet, there's no knowing where you might be swept off to."

It's a dangerous business, going out your front door.

Eventually, we got unstuck. The tow truck came and tugged Willie out, a smooth extraction, like the pulling of a baby tooth. At 10:35 pm that Sunday night, I sat down and blogged about the whole experience. The generator hummed under the bus. The kids slept in their bunks. Maile was asleep back in the bedroom. And I sat out front, listening to the heat go on and off, listening to The National, listening.

Sometimes that's the only way to get unstuck, I guess. Just stop and listen.

Stuck

"The fear of death follows from the fear of life. A man who lives fully is prepared to die at any time."

Mark Twain

So we headed south through Virginia along Route 81, a highway that slips in and out of the foothills of the mountains. The road there is like a sliver of thread dropped amongst rocks, and it winds along the path of least resistance. Already, we had left Pennsylvania and Maryland and a small piece of West Virginia behind us.

Towards the end of what felt like a very long day, we came down the east side of a gradual mountainside somewhere south of Harrisonburg. Trees lined the highway, a sea of ash brown interspersed with the occasional drooping evergreen. The sun set behind us, pushing the bus's shadow far in front, all the way into eternity.

North-facing banks held up a thick layer of snow – the south-facing banks looked soggy and water-logged. It was like driving the line between two seasons.

Sammy and Abra slept in their bunks. Cade and Lucy read quietly at the back of the bus. Maile wrote at the dining table just behind my right shoulder.

One of my favorite songs came on, Tom Petty singing a slow version of "King's Highway":

Oh I await the day
Good fortune comes our way
And we ride down the king's highway

Off to the right side of the highway, something came into view under the drifting shadows of the evergreens and planted firmly in the midst of the snow. It was one of those roadside memorials, mounds of flowers lying in bunches and handwritten notes stapled or tacked to a white, handmade cross.

In an instant, was the thought that went through my mind. *Those things happen in an instant.*

But as the bus drew closer and then flew past the marker, my last glance caught sight of a hand-painted sign attached to the bottom of the cross. It was one word, in neatly painted black letters on a white background. Just a name.

Sammy.

Later during that drive, Sammy, my 2-year-old Sammy, came wandering up the aisle in the bus and sat with Maile at the table. He leaned over the back of the booth, looked forward through the bus's huge windscreen, sucking his thumb and holding on to his blanket.

"You drive the bus?" he asked me. He always asks that.

"That's right, buddy. I'm driving the bus."

And I was thankful that my Sammy sat there with me, sucking his thumb and watching the road. I was thankful for this opportunity. I was even thankful for a stuck bus and another 9,000 miles.

42

"Travel is fatal to prejudice, bigotry, and narrow-mindedness, and many of our people need it sorely on these accounts. Broad, wholesome, charitable views of men and things cannot be acquired by vegetating in one little corner of the earth all one's lifetime."

Mark Twain

We walked through the woods to the large clearing. A barely discernible wall surrounded the area where the slaves had been buried. At the far corner, small fluorescent orange and blue flags stood perched at attention, marking excavation already completed.

It all felt as haunted as any place I've ever been. But haunted isn't exactly the word – inhabited? Unbearably heavy? Having been mostly forgotten but itself never forgetting? That's the feeling the leaf-covered plot of space in the woods gave me.

"How old are you, Cade?" Andi, a friend from college and our tour guide of the estate in central Virginia, asked my oldest son.

"Eight," he said proudly.

"Hmmm," she said. "At eight years old, a slave was expected to hoe in the fields from sunup to sundown."

Cade's eyes went wide. I stare at his frail, thin arms. I try not to imagine the sunburn that would have covered his narrow shoulders, the blisters bubbling out between his fingers during that first week of being eight years old and working so hard.

"And how old are you, Lucy?" she asked.

"I'm seven," Lucy said quietly.

"It would be your job to stay behind all day and watch the little children," Andi said to her quietly. This said to Lucy, the lovely girl who spends most of her days reading, or imagining, or being what she is: a child.

Only a handful of gravestones still stood in that clearing, even though well over 100 slaves lived, worked, and died there. So we made our way methodically through one of the corners of the graveyard, poking thin metal rods into the soft earth, fishing for stones that may have fallen over and been covered with dirt and debris during the intervening 150 years.

Thunk. My metal rod tapped against something. I moved it three inches to the side. Thunk. Again. Thunk. I called Andi over. We dug carefully with our hands, pulled away the dirt, ripped out the

44

roots of weeds and grass. 150 years of debris. And there it was: the edge of what looked like a quartz rock.

"Quartz isn't native to this area," Andi said. "This is probably the edge of a footstone."

We marked the area with a colorful blue flag. Later, Andi would expose more of the stone, brush away the dust, exhume the past.

That night, when the sun had set and our stomachs were full from dinner, we walked out and started a fire. The kids melted marshmallows and made s'mores. Andi, her father, Maile and I mostly sat and talked, enjoyed the warmth, smiled at the children.

At one point, I leaned my head back and look up into that sky, immeasurable. Stars stared down. It caught me unawares, the realization that the slaves buried in that graveyard once looked up at the same sky, the same stars. Many of them had given birth to their children in a dark night such as that one. Many of them had exhaled their last breath under those same constellations. The molecules that made up their bodies were there, all around me.

And to be honest, I didn't know what to do with that, because as I let my soul touch just the edge of that cold, mostly buried rock of injustice, my throat ached and constricted, and my eyes felt heavy and inhabited by too much emotion.

Immeasurable.

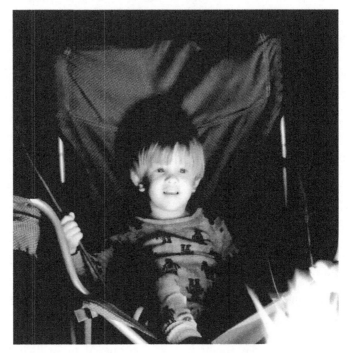

Sam enjoying the smores and the fire.

"I pack my trunk, embrace my friends, embark on the sea and at last wake up in Naples, and there beside me is the stern fact, the sad self, unrelenting, identical, that I fled from."

Ralph Waldo Emerson

The bus pulled lazily along the bottom edge of the valley, leaving the slave graveyard behind, as well as two people and a dog who suddenly felt very much like family: Andi, her father Woody, and their dog Caruso.

Just the night before, Abra and Sammy had run across the room and leaped up into Woody's arms, and he had built a fire so that they could roast marshmallows. Then, on that very morning, as we had slept, he had placed a connected hose beside the bus so that I could fill up the fresh water tank. Later, as we prepared the bus for departure, he had taken the kids, one by one, on a tractor ride, during which it was impossible to decide who enjoyed themselves more: Woody or the children.

But that was behind us. To the left of the stone drive: thick woods and a steep hill, an introduction to the rolling land of Bremo Bluff. To the right, and the south, lay an often-traveled train track, then a wide expanse of marshy flatness, then a tree-covered incline. The bus protested as we pulled out on to Route 15, but soon enough we were rolling.

Tom Petty sang on the radio as we drove away:

When the time gets right
I'm gonna pick you up
And take you far away
From trouble my love

Under a big old sky
Out in a field of green
There's gotta be something
Left for us to believe

The hills grew shallower towards Appomattox, or at least they seemed to, as if someone had pulled on both sides of an unruly sheet. The fields were a golden tan, looked like harvest seven months early, but the naked trees gave them away. Nearly 147 years ago, General Robert E. Lee signed surrender documents in that county after realizing his forces were hopelessly outnumbered.

If I didn't know its history, would I still think those hills exuded a somber hue, the taste of a proud resignation? I sensed little defeat there – rather, it felt like the epicenter of some new kind of unity.

Then, the Eagles started singing:

There are stars
In the Southern sky
Southward as you go
There is moonlight
And moss in the trees
Down the Seven Bridges Road

Hours later, North Carolina welcomed us with heavy winds, a spitting rain, and a sudden drop in temperature. The kids grew antsy as we reached, and then exceeded, our longest drive to date, around 300 miles. Maile and I spent a long time talking about our future after this trip, where our lives were headed, where we might end up.

Massive rays of sunshine slanted down through storm clouds, and it was impossible to tell if the windshield was wet from rain or water coming up off the highway. We were somewhere north of Raleigh. I turned to Maile, looked at her through all of the stress and anxiety and worry that had risen during that first week on the road. She looked at me, and it was as if we suddenly saw ourselves. We were like spoiled children, whining about things not being easy enough.

I smiled.

"If we don't work on changing our attitudes, this is going to be a long four months."

She laughed.

"I was thinking the exact same thing."

We decided in that moment to, as much as possible, see every challenge from there on out as an inevitable part of the adventure. No matter what. So Willie rolled into Charlotte, where we would stay with Maile's parents for almost a week. It would be a welcome timeout, a much-needed break from showering on the bus and operating in cramped quarters.

But even in light of such determination to chill out, I continued to worry. And a body is not designed to operate under that kind of stress for very long. The mental anxiety turned into a physical problem that almost grounded us in North Carolina.

> **"Adventure, yeah. I guess that's what you call it when everybody comes back alive."**
>
> **Mercedes Lackey**

I sat on the bathroom floor. It was 1am, and the worst stomach pains I had ever felt came and went like contractions. I wished there was something I could deliver from my body that would rid me of the rhythmic pain, but nothing worked. I stared at the toilet, held my stomach, and moaned.

Before long, I stumbled back to the bedroom and got on my knees beside the bed because it was the only comfortable position I could find. Then, I lay my face down and drifted in and out of sleep for the next two hours.

At 3am, another sharp pain woke me up. I was exhausted, and we were supposed to leave Charlotte later that day, but unless this thing got resolved, there was no way I could drive. I stumbled into the bathroom again and filled the bath with water as hot as I could bear.

Outside, thunder rumbled in the distance. I turned out the bathroom light, climbed into the bath, and leaned back. Lightning flashed across the window, closely followed by another blast of thunder. The house shook in the storm. Rain pelted the window so hard that it sounded like hail.

Slowly, the pains subsided. I took deep breaths. I tried to meditate. I tried to relax. I fell asleep in the tub.

When I woke up a few minutes later, I felt slightly better, but very weak. I dried off and walked gingerly to the bed. Lightning flashed again, sending white light through the room, illuminating the windows. I pulled myself in deep under the blankets. After a few moments, I fell asleep.

The pain subsided over the next few days and gradually vanished over the coming weeks. It was a challenge to me to stop holding on to stress. I needed to spend more time listening, more time in the moment, and less time obsessing over what might go wrong.

"No, no! The adventures first, explanations take such a dreadful time."

Lewis Carroll

Saturday morning. I sat down in Willie's huge driver's seat and took a deep breath. We had about three hours to our next destination, Orange Park, Florida, and all the little zoo animals (aka children) were fed, watered, and ready to go. We had spent the night at a truck stop close to Orangeburg, SC and were parked between two huge 18-wheelers. It was actually kind of a cozy spot.

It was the first of many nights we spent at truck stops. Truck stops had scared me when I was a kid – I imagined everyone there was either a murderer, a professional child abductor, or a drug trafficker. Turns out that my rather egregious stereotyping was completely wrong – we met many kind people at truck stops. These gathering places began to have the feel of a watering hole, where all the animals stop for nourishment, rest, and a bit of quiet.

53

Anyway, that next morning we woke up to rain. The storms that went on to wreak so much havoc later in the day were passing through – the hurricanes stayed to the north of us, but heavy bands of precipitation pounded the roof and windows of the bus.

It was time to head further south. I turned the bus key to "on" and pushed the red button. Nothing. Uh-oh. This had happened once or twice before, and all I had to do was jump-start it with our van, but I didn't want to go outside. Not in that weather. I looked at all the buttons again, wondering if I had left something running overnight that drained the battery. I turned the key off and on again. Pushed the button. Not even a click.

Oh, man. The ran was pouring down in sheets. I couldn't find my raincoat, so I put on a heavy, corduroy number created more for cold, dry, Pennsylvania winters than for warm, humid, tropical storm-like conditions. I put on a baseball cap. I tried to put on a good attitude.

Fortunately, the jumper cables reached from the mini-van we towed behind to the bus battery. I did all the hooking up, turned on the van, went back into the bus, and turned it on. Pushed the button. Nothing.

I went back outside and did what my driver's education teacher told us never to do: I banged the live ends of the jumper cables together to see if I had a spark. Nothing. *What is going on?* I'll tell

54

you what was going on – I was getting more and more wet. Soaked. I went back in to the bus to try one more time. That's when I noticed something.

The bus was still in drive.

So the night before I must have parked, turned off the bus, and put on the parking brake. But I never put it back into neutral (there is no "park").

I smiled to myself. Really, I did, right there on the over-sized driver's seat with water dripping from the bill of my baseball cap, right there with my fake wool coat that weighed as much as an entire sheep. And this question entered my mind, right there at a truck stop in South Carolina.

How often is my life in drive when it should be in neutral?

I know, I know. All the big life gurus talk about how important drive is, how indispensable the go-get-'em disposition. And of course, there is always a time for that dogged determination to make something happen.

But sometimes I feel like that's all I'm ever doing. Drive, drive, drive. Push for this book deal, make another call about that project, write, write, write. Then, I wonder why things don't start up the way I want them to. I wonder why nothing happens, no matter how many ways I try to jump-start an idea, or a business plan, or a direction in life.

Maybe I just need to put things back in neutral.

"The past is never where you think you left it."

Katharine Anne Porter

"Isn't that where we used to turn?" Maile asked.

We were too late – the sun had already set in Orange Park, Florida. Still, we drove our minivan on dark streets through the vaguely familiar neighborhood.

"I think that's the road," Maile would say, or, "Wait, that looks familiar."

Then, as if emerging from a dream: clarity. Turn right at the stop sign. Straight through the next intersection. Then finally left on to Papaya Drive.

Even without the sun, the sky maintained some kind of cobalt blue against which the inky outlines of palm trees made everything feel very foreign, very faraway, and very long ago. I stopped the van and put it in park. Maile and I stared across the street at the single story house.

Twelve and a half years had passed, but nothing had changed. Oh, maybe a tree was missing from the front yard. Maybe the grass looked better cared for. I doubted that an anemic vegetable garden resided behind the house.

Memories popped into my mind like Polaroids. Pulling up all the carpet in the living room during our first day there and then sleeping on the rolls of old carpet that night. Me coming home from a long week on the road to find light peeking around the edges of the curtains, knowing the person who loved me most on this earth sat inside that house. Bringing home a little puppy that totally cramped our style but to whom we could not say, "no."

And they just kept flashing through my mind, these moments.

But sitting there in the minivan, with four kids crying or laughing or arguing in the back seats, it felt like maybe all that stuff had never happened. And if it did happen, it was so long ago – maybe it didn't matter. Maybe all those memories would eventually just evaporate from my brain, and then from Maile's brain, and then all would be forgotten. Then, Maile reached over and grabbed my hand.

"It's been a crazy 12 ½ years," she said, and I knew exactly what she meant. And suddenly it did matter, every little moment, even the ones I'd already forgotten because all of those prior moments brought us to that moment, parked in the dark in a minivan with our four audacious children having their own Barnum and Bailey's three-ring circus in the back seats.

So we parked there, our headlights shining down that old familiar road, and we stared at that house the way you stare at an old friend when you pass them at the county fair, and then, you walk on without saying anything because words would only ruin the ground around the memorials of those good times. Some things are best left in the very long ago.

"A good traveler has no fixed plans and is not intent on arriving."

Lao Tzu

After an evening of reminiscing and a subsequent morning of errand running in Orange Park, we readied Willie for the short jaunt to Gainesville, our next stop. As it seemed his thirst was never fully quenched, his tank needed attending to before we could hit the road. We squeezed the bus into a narrow, conventional gas station. Maile got out and peered up to make sure we didn't clip the overhang. I put on the parking break, then filled the tank with $400 worth of diesel. Ouch.

My main concern at that point became our exit route: used cars lined the back of the gas station parking lot, but I couldn't cut the corner too close or the minivan we towed behind would hit the gas pump and blow up the entire city. It had become interesting to me on this trip, though, how just when we think we have all the potential pitfalls in life identified, something completely random

60

happens. Something we never could have imagined. Something immeasurably random.

Something like the ignition falling into the dashboard.

I sat in the driver's seat holding the bus key in my hand, staring at the new hole in the dash, perfectly round. I would not have felt any more shocked if a rabbit followed the ignition through the hole, shouting, "I'm late! I'm late!"

An empty hole. Where the ignition used to be. My first response (not usually the smartest one) immediately shouted, *Quick, reach in there and grab it!* So I stuck my index finger into the hole. And my finger got stuck.

Maile stood outside the bus, waiting to help me navigate the minefield of used cars and gas pumps. She looked at me impatiently. What was taking so long? Why hadn't I started the bus? I waved her inside. She opened the bus door.

"What are you laughing at?" she asked.

"The ignition just fell into the dashboard, and now my finger is stuck," I said, laughter erupting out of me. She looked at me as if I had lost touch with reality.

"What?!"

Just then I gave a mighty pull and yanked my finger out. A thick layer of skin around my knuckle fell down into the dash, joining the ignition. Now what? We scrambled around the bus looking for a flashlight; then, I shouted out to one of the gas station attendants that it might be a little while before we left. She gave me a blank look, swept up a few more cigarette butts, then, shrugged her shoulders. Permission to not go anywhere? Granted.

I aimed the flashlight down the hole. The ignition and its accompanying wires rested three or four inches below where it should have been. I got on my back below the steering wheel and peered up. I could just about see it through the undergrowth of wires and connectors and thingamabobs. Maile gave me a chopstick, and I tried to push the ignition up – she sat poised with tweezers, a domesticated Mr. Miyagi, waiting to snag it. Nothing worked.

Eventually, I found a few small screws and took them out. That particular piece of dash popped off. The ignition fit right back into its rightful place.

Improvisation.

Cooperation

Laughter.

Tools we would use more and more as this trip progressed.

"Adventures do occur, but not punctually."
E.M. Forster

As soon as this trip was planned back in December, Abra somehow got wind that her birthday would be taking place in Florida. She proceeded to remind us of this fact every…single…day. So when the day finally arrived, in Gainesville, Florida on March 5th, we were all worked into a lather about it: the Bigs (Cade and Lucy) were eager to shower her with presents, Sammy was eager to open all her presents, and we, the parents, watched, feeling bittersweet towards the vision of our flopsy little girl inching further away from babyhood.

With the urging of the Bigs, we got her a Barbie laptop for her birthday, this chintzy hot pink contraption with computer graphics fresh from the eighties. When she opened the present, we squealed with delight, gushing about how fantastic it was; she just stood there and smiled that goofy old smile of hers. I think we could have wrapped up a box of toothpicks, and she would have been just as pleased. It was the sheer joy of a birthday that sustained her. "I just love birthdays," she said later that day. "Birthdays are the best thing ever!"

Later on the morning of Abra's birthday, a young lady drove up next to our minivan, rolled down her window, and peered through the passenger side.

"Shawn?"

I got out of the van, walked around, and gave her a big hug, because even though we'd never met in person, I felt like I knew her. This was Tamára of "Tamára Out Loud" fame, and I was happy to meet her. She was just as full of life and kindness as her writing makes her out to be.

What a day she had in store for us.

We walked for miles through a beautiful park, the kids searching for alligators and cranes while Maile, Tamára,, and I talked about life and parenthood and writing. From there we had lunch at The Swamp, a Gainesville institution. And if you read Tamára's blog, you know the day wouldn't be complete unless we did something illegal, so we went to this huge wall in Gainesville that everyone paints. The kids added their own layer of graffiti.

That night we waited until dusk and then watched thousands and thousands of bats fly from a bat house to the lake, right over our heads, each of them trying to avoid the lone hawk picking them off one at a time.

Tamára took me to a coffee shop that night and introduced me to three of her creative friends. We talked about our goals and what keeps us from reaching them. We talked about the importance of reading well. We didn't realize what time it was until the barista turned off the lights, a not-so-subtle hint that we had stayed past the 11pm closing.

This became one of my favorite parts of the trip: bolstering these online friendships with hugs or handshakes. Jake and Shawna Lewis, Andi Cumbo, Stacy Barton, Tamára Lunardo, Eric Wyatt, Matthew Paul Turner, an entire host of writers at The Killer Tribe's Conference in Nashville, Lore Ferguson, Jennifer Luitwieler, Jason Boyett, Heather Fishman, and Kristin Tennant: these folks took time out for our family. Some even made us a meal and introduced us to their writer friends.

It's a great big world out there, full of people like you.

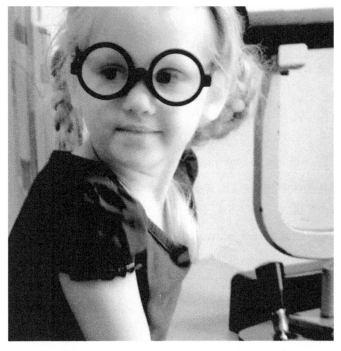

Abra practicing to be an eye doctor during a visit to one of the many children's museums we frequented on our trip.

"I travel a lot; I hate having my life disrupted by routine."

Caskie Stinnett

On Tuesday, Willie took to the road, headed south to Orlando, Florida. In one of her blog posts, Maile gave her perspective on that particular travel day:

Yesterday, A Walmart somewhere in Gainesville, 8:30 a.m.

The stench from our bathroom set the schedule for our day's activities: our waste tank needed dumping and fast. So Shawn set about hooking the van to the trailer at the back of Willie, while I fed the kids their requisite bowl of cereal and secured all drawers and cupboards before our "home on wheels" got moving.

This is one of my favorite parts of a "traveling day." I imagine myself as a flight attendant in a neatly tailored skirt and blouse (in a sensible color like navy) with sturdy yet elegant high heels walking purposefully along the narrow thoroughfare of our bus, fastening the metal latches on each compartment, the resolute "click" that says "ready for take-off." I think I even wear a rather smug look on my face while I'm "preparing the cabin," though I haven't yet looked in the mirror to see for sure.

The kids each find an activity to occupy them during the drive, anywhere from Barbies to Matchbox cars to annoying everyone in arm's reach (Sammy's specialty). I perch beside Shawn on the cushy "co-pilot" seat up front, and we're off. When we first started this adventure, the moment the bus lurched forward on its trek, my stomach would immediately begin doing advanced yoga poses in my gut. But that was almost 3 weeks ago; now it's just life as usual. I kick my feet up on the dash, and we listen to James Taylor and look like old pros.

About 30 minutes later, we stopped in Ocala at a dingy little establishment called "Holiday Trav L Park." Clever. Shawn shoehorned Willie down the narrow, black-topped pathway that led to the dump station. Now, let me just tell you that there is nothing on earth that makes a person feel more like an animal than watching all their bodily waste rush down a red accordion tube into the metal opening of a sewage receptacle. Sheesh, you could smell us a mile away. While for the past 12 years I have felt my love for my husband increase day by day, it absolutely gushes forth from every pore of my body like Old Faithful when I see him emptying our waste tank. This man is indeed a keeper.

After we lightened our load, Willie set his sights on Oakland, Florida, just on the outskirts of Orlando. Our friend Renault pastors a congregation there, and they are graciously allowing Willie to camp out for 3 days in their church's front lawn.

Upon arrival, we released the hounds (aka, our children) to play in the clearing beside Willie while I put together a light lunch of peppers, strawberries, and yogurt.

With bellies full and eyelids heavy, we all retired to our respective bunks for an afternoon siesta. And that, folks, was the best sleep I've had on this entire trip. The wind lazily blew through the open bedroom window, keeping the air fresh but not cold; I didn't even need a sheet to cover me.

I admit I went to sleep heavy-minded. This trip has brought up so many questions for me as well as reflections on the past that confuse and sometimes frustrate me. But on the breeze floating through the window, my burdens seemed to be whisked away and I awoke feeling lighter.

Ah, Sleep: the Great Restorer.

After we spent the afternoon getting situated and resting, I [Shawn] drove into Orlando to meet my writer friend Stacy Barton in person for the first time.

Again, what a night! We met at a wine bar, and as soon as I saw Stacy, I felt like I was seeing an old friend. We talked for about thirty minutes before the others arrived, here and there, one at a time. Even my good friend Janet Oberholtzer, in town for a race and some book talks, was able to be there. We drank wine and ate cheese and bread, and everyone was so refreshingly honest about their recent disappointments, their hopes, and their pending potential successes.

Not only that, but I got to meet Billy Collins, 2-term United States poet laureate and a recent presenter of a TED talk. He told me stories of when he joined Garrison Keillor on *Prairie Home Companion*, and what it's like to write in Florida versus writing in New York, where he grew up. One of the most encouraging things he said to me that night came after he asked me how old I was.

"35," I said. He sort of looked at me as if I had just been born last week.

"Well," he said slowly. "I didn't really make it anywhere as a poet until I was in my mid-40s."

"That's every encouraging," I said.

"It should be," he replied with a huge smile.

But while I spent my time meeting a poet laureate and receiving his encouragement, Maile experienced life a little differently. Yet, somehow we both ended up feeling encouraged

Yesterday presented a wonderful opportunity for me to experience the joys of my children in lesser denominations. In the morning, the "Littles" (Abra and Sam) joined me on my errand running around the delightful town of Winter Garden, FL. They wrestled in the aisles of the RV parts department as I attempted to explain to a rather flabbergasted sales lady that indeed our "gray and black water holding tanks are one in the same". (That's RV-speak for "we poop and shower into the same container under our bus". Telling from the appalled look on her face, this is rather exceptional in camping circles.)

From there, we visited the public restrooms at the RV sales lot, where I repeatedly shouted, "Yucka!" at Sam as he persisted in perusing the wall-mounted, feminine hygiene receptacle, lifting it's metal lid up and down, a goofy smile on his face. He thought it was a game; I most certainly did not.

Then, we got lost in our attempt to find Target, during which I continued to hear shouts from the back of the van, issuing various commentaries, questions and demands.

Sam: "I want candy!"

Me: "Well, if you are a good listener, we can get some gum at Target."

Sam: "I want gum!"

Abra: "I wish I had a nice mama!"

Me: "Me, too."

Abra: "Just kigging [kidding]! I love you, Mama! You are the best mama in the whole world."

Me: "I love you too, Punky."

Abra: "Now when are we are going to be there? This is taking forever!"

Me: "I totally agree."

After we found Target and diapers and gum, I deposited the "Littles" back at the bus with Shawn for their naptime and picked up the "Bigs" (Cade and Lucy) for an afternoon at the Orlando Science Center.

What a different experience. The 25-minute drive to the museum was peacefully quiet, with Cade sharing the occasional punch-line from the comic strip book he was reading. When we got to the parking lot, everyone unbuckled him/herself; no one sat on the oil-stained concrete floor in retaliation for not being carried or screamed when they didn't press the Level 2 elevator button in time.

When we entered the museum, each of us spoke at normal decibels; no need to warn anyone about "inside voices." In the restroom, everyone wiped themselves and steered clear of the used sanitary napkins. When I asked them to come to an exhibit I thought was interesting, they didn't giggle and dart in the opposite direction. They were, simply, more grown up. And I appreciated that.

Through the alligator and stingray exhibits, I watched my children ask thoughtful questions and make keen observations. They politely thanked the elderly nature guide who allowed them to pet her baby alligator. With an equal portion of intrigue and fear, they studied the skeletons of a T-rex and Triceratops.

One exhibit explained how to determine the age of a tree. All three of us stared with open mouths as we looked at the cross-section of a 300 year old tree.

"Mom, will the redwoods be bigger than this?" Cade asked.

"Oh, yeah," I smiled. "A lot bigger." And suddenly I couldn't wait to be standing at the base of one of those majestic wonders, introducing my children to one of the oldest living things they will ever see.

As we studied the hundreds of rings, following them down to the center like a funnel of time, my eyes focused on a dark, solitary spot in the middle: a sapling began this beautiful giant.

We all come from humble beginnings. We all start as "Littles."

"So I learned two things that night, and the next day, from him: the perfection of a moment, and the fleeting nature of it."

Margaret George

I sat at the small booth towards the front of the bus spreading brie on crackers and eating them in between sentences – such delicious punctuation. It was a muggy space, there inside the bus, with too few windows to let in the cool Orlando night. So we rigged fans to circulate air, everyone drank lots of cold water, and Sam fell asleep in his new spot on the floor beside our bed, sweat dampening the hair around his ears.

Willie sat in the vacant lot beside our friend's church outside of Orlando. We could have been the last people on the planet, with our dark window shades and the generator beneath us that drowned out all sound. But then my phone lit up with an incoming message, like Morse code or a pulse from deep space, and I knew that we were not the last.

74

I could see Maile at the end of the long hall, her face glowing white while she typed.

A picture surprised me as I scrolled through my phone, a photo of our chickens' secret egg stash at our old house. For perhaps three minutes, I stared at that pile of riddles, like an archeologist finding proof of some long ago culture hidden amidst the chaos of vines and beetles. That had been our life once. And not "once" as in ten years before, though that's what it felt like. This "once" meant simply three weeks and two days ago. Not even a month. Not even a lunar cycle.

It scared me, how fast things had changed.

We build our little castles in the sand and we dig and we sweat and, with painstaking tedium, we articulate the details. We carve out the moats and areas to carry away the water we know will come. We try to protect our creations with high walls and deep ditches.

But the tide always returns, pulled in by a moon we can barely see. And the sand we have accumulated can never withstand it.

Yet, somehow we find the space to build anyway, to construct these castles in spite of what we know, regardless of their fleeting nature. Because as we build we realize it's not about the sand. It's not about the way the walls melt under the first crashing waves. It's not about what we lose.

It's about the strength we gain in our fingers. It's about callouses that begin to layer on our palms. It's about the creativity and the perseverance and the fortitude infused into each new structure.

It's not about the castle. It never has been. It's about us.

I looked back the long hall towards where the kids held their books out over the edges of their bunks, showing each other what they worked on or read. Abra's hair floated around her flushed face in wispy ringlets. Cade and Lucy opened each of their curtains to feel the cool air from the fan.

I turned out the lights and followed the flashlight back to bed.

**"Now more than ever do I realize that I will never be content
with a sedentary life, that I will always be haunted by
thoughts of a sun-drenched elsewhere."**

Isabelle Eberhardt

Maile

It seemed our waste always kept us on the move. Before leaving
our cozy spot just outside of Orlando, the waste pipes in Willie's
belly clued us in that our dump tank was at its limit. So we quickly
readied the bus for departure, did a quick internet search for the
closest dump station, and barreled down the road.

After relieving Willie, we forged on to Sarasota, the next scheduled
stop on our trip. We were meeting Shawn's family there while
resting Willie's weary bones at a shady little campsite in the Amish
resort of Pinecraft. When we nestled into that tidy little spot and
turned off Willie's engine at the beginning of our 10-day stay, I
wondered if I'd ever want to leave. It felt good to stay in one spot

for a while, surrounded by people you know and love, cocooned in safety. But surprisingly, I never had to summon the will to move on; it came naturally in the form of an unmistakable itch:

This morning, after the Bigs left for the beach with their grandparents and the Littles battled their way into naptime, Shawn sat at the kitchen table, writing, while I stood at the stove, brewing up another batch of Ham and Bean Soup.

"I'm ready to get outta here," he said, glancing up at me, smiling and thoughtful. I grinned back because he had echoed exactly the feeling that greeted my waking eyes earlier this morning. I had been laying in bed, nestled under the minimal protection of a sheet as a coolish breeze blew through Willie's only openable (is that a word?) window, when the sensation hit: it's time to move on.

Our visit in Sarasota has been everything we needed it to be: late-night card games with family, slow bike rides on overgrown tricycles, unflinching sunshine, and ten consecutive nights of ice cream after dinner, simple ingredients for an unforgettable week.

But I'm getting an itch, somewhere towards the tops of my shoulders, almost at the base of my neck. It's the itch to move on. I've gotten more familiar with the sensation as our trip goes along. Once the novelty of a place wears off, my mind begins to wander to other spaces, locations in my mental sphere that I don't want it to go, places like "Where-Will-We-Move-to-When-the-Trip-is-Over-ville", "Not-Good-Enough Beach", "Anxiety-over-Money City" and "What-Kind-of-Children-am-I-Raising-burg." Our traveling is a necessary and delightful distraction.

Years and years ago, a counselor introduced me to the concept of "ruminating."
It may be hard to believe, but even at the blossoming age of twelve, I had
already developed the habit of cozying up with my thoughts, sorting through
them like baseball cards, memorizing the sub-A grade on a test or reliving a
cold interaction with my dad, for days, weeks, even years.

Now, the details of my thoughts have changed and multiplied, but my reaction
to them hasn't. Too often I live in my mind, traipsing through the muddy streets
and across the rickety bridges to the thoughts that have built awkward,
fumbling cities of "what if's" and "not good enoughs." Sure, I'll go through the
routine of life, but I spend too much time residing, living, in my mind.

However, as this trip progresses, there have been too many exciting, life-giving
activities going on that I can't manage to set up shop in my mind. The magnetic
pull of real life is too much for the pathetic whispers of the shriveled cities in my
mind. And that's a really good thing. But I do start to wonder, "Maile, what
will you do when this trip ends? What will you do when you can't just pull up
stakes the moment things get mundane and you start doing the rounds at your
mental hot-spots? Are you creating a bad habit here?"

I'm not sure, but I'm going to take the "cup is half-full" approach on this one
and say, "No." I think I actually may be creating some helpful habits of how
to deal with the wanderings of my mind from here on out. Perhaps, when this
adventure ends, I'll just start a new one. I wonder if maybe I didn't fill my real
life with enough gusto to make it worth staying in. In the past, I equated a good
day with laundry done and folded, kids bathed, house vacuumed, kitchen
cleaned, and 30 minutes of quiet time for myself.

Really? Is a neat and tidy life equal to a life well lived? Let's just say, I'm beginning to have my doubts...

Abra playing on the beach at Siesta Key, Florida during a storm-laden sunset. Later we found her making sand-angels, fully clothed. She is our child who embraces life in all of its messiness.

> "Everybody has to leave, everybody has to leave their home and come back so they can love it again for all new reasons."

Donald Miller

I had my own wrestling match with normalcy and comfort. The blue bus relaxed in the shade of tall trees on a small back street in a quiet suburb. A thick electrical cord wound its way to a 30-amp socket, meaning the generator (aka the old man under the bus) could rest. A wide tube exited from the bus's innards and trailed into a septic tank, meaning the waste can be emptied at any time. That little spot under the trees was a comfortable place.

At night, we would turn on three small fans. One pulled cool air in through the only bus window that opened. The second one, situated in the hall, pushed the cool air up to Cade's bunk. Lucy hoarded the third fan in the top bunk, where the air was warmest. When the lights blinked off, the sound of the three fans created a trio of white noise, lullabies of refreshing air that sang us all to sleep. We woke up in the morning cold, wrapped in blankets we hadn't thought we'd ever need again.

It was the most comfortable spot we'd been in during our entire trip. No need to drive anywhere. No diesel required to run the bus. Palm trees on the other side of the street waved their fronds up and down, up and down, moving in the sweeping drift of a hypnotist's locket and chain. The leaning trees whispered to us:

"You are feeling very sleepy. You're eyelids are growing heavy. Now count slowly backwards from ten to one. Repeat after me: this is a comfortable place. This is a comfortable place. I do not want to leave this place."

Palm trees can be very convincing.

Comfort is a funny thing. We aim for it. We strive for it. We work hard to attain it. So much of what we do in life is centered around becoming comfortable. I eat because I don't like the discomfort of feeling hungry. I sleep to ward off weariness. I work to make money so that I can have nice things that make my life easier or more fun.

And I don't think there's anything wrong with that.

But comfort brings new problems. Comfort attained often inhibits growth. It distracts us from setting or reaching new goals. Having grown comfortable, we stop learning about ourselves. In the end, comfort makes us rigid and inflexible in our thinking.

If we're not careful, the refusal to relinquish existing comforts derails dreams and places us on paths with other unsavory travelers: namely, Boredom and Ineffective Living.

It would have been silly to live the rest of our lives on a bus parked on a small street in Pinecraft just because we didn't want to give up those comforts. Think of all the sights we would have missed out on! Think of all the people we would never have met! Think of all the annoying adventures we wouldn't have had to deal with!

Don't let comfort keep you from living. Don't let the fear of discomfort keep you camped on a back street of life. Don't be scared to disconnect, batten down the hatches, and hit the road, if that's where your journey leads you.

"The real voyage of discovery consists not in seeking new landscapes, but in having new eyes."

Marcel Proust

So we left Florida and headed north. That leg from Sarasota to Nashville would be the last stretch we were relatively familiar with – after that, it was all new and fresh and untrodden territory. We planned two stops: one at a state park in Georgia, and the other in the outskirts of Atlanta. We were glad to be on the road again.

I felt better about driving the bus. Confidence began creeping up around the corners of my driving – I may have even begun passing people on the highway at this point. Filling up with gas and emptying the waste tank no longer filled me with apprehension. We learned that we were still malleable, changeable, and we adapted to life on the road. Of course, this all took about four weeks.

The kids, meanwhile, acted as if they had never lived anywhere else. When we stopped at playgrounds, they chatted with the other children. When we went to bed, they found their favorite books and seemed glad for the privacy of their bunks. They played or watched movies in the back room, seemingly oblivious to the fact that the bus they sat in sped along at 65 mph.

Maile made some interesting observations about them in this blog post:

I remember as a child often wondering why my mom was so boring.

I'd stand at the edge of the Troy Municipal Swimming Pool, preparing to do a cannonball, and glance back to see her stretched out on a lounge chair, reading a book. Incomprehensible. Why would a person with functional arms and legs actually choose to sit solitary, reading, when all the excitement of an over-chlorinated and over-populated swimming pool lay ten feet away. Turds bobbing near the drainage spout and lip-locked teenagers wouldn't deter me for a second. There was adventure to be had in those fluorescent blue waters.

I'd long given up trying to coax my mom to join me. "No, you go ahead and play with your friends. I'm just gonna sit here and read," she'd respond with a smile. So off I'd run after my pals and make the mental promise that I would never be that way when I grew up.

Fast forward about 25 years and who is that woman in the matronly swimming suit, draped over a beach chair, dozing (and perhaps drooling) in the sun? Yep, it's me.

Now I, like my mother so many years ago, sit on the beach, cursing the sand and pooh-poohing all the requests from my children to "help me make a sandcastle" or "splash in the water with me." All the frivolity is simply too taxing for me. I hide under my sunhat,, avoiding eye contact and playing deaf with anyone under the age of 20.

How did this happen? When did I make this evolution from the frolicking child to the boondocked mama? I'll tell you exactly when it happened: 8 ½ years ago when I became the mother of a blue-eyed little baby boy. From that moment on, he, and our children that would follow him, slowly soaked up the child that I had been. In 24 years of life, I'd created quite a sea of energy, sleep, and creativity. And they, like 4 gigantic sponges, laid themselves upon my surface and started absorbing, till what is now left is a quickly evaporating puddle leftover after a mid-summer rain.

I love that the child in me is carried on in them. I smile as I watch their spindly, pale arms packing down buckets of wet sand to build castle walls the way I did decades ago. I laugh as they discover the warm thrill of peeing in the ocean, a tactic I often used to take the chill off the icy waves. Still, I look forward to the day when my puddle increases again as they, one by one, wring out their sponges to create a vast sea for children of their own, just as my mom created an ocean for me.

But until then, I'll tend my weary puddle with sun-bathed naps and ample sunscreen...and wait patiently for the rainy season.

> "I have found out that there ain't no surer way to find out whether you like people or hate them than to travel with them."
>
> — Mark Twain

Maile

The day before we left Reed Bingham State Park, Shawn walked into the bedroom after spending the afternoon writing at a coffee shop and found me lying on the couch looking crazy-eyed. He tenderly suggested, "Why don't you go have some time to yourself…"

This has become our new, and necessary, habit. Spending the day hanging out in a bus with 4 lively children can bring a mother to the edge. So I threw on some shoes and rushed out the door before anyone could ask for a drink or need a diaper change.

I knew exactly where I wanted to go. The first day we arrived there, one of the park employees had given me a map of the area with a detailed drawing of some trails about a ½ mile north of where we were camping. I needed some space and nature to clear my mind; those trails would do the trick.

As I ran down the road leading to the trails, I felt the slightest sense of apprehension. These trails were secluded, nothing else around but forest and prairie. I hadn't told Shawn where I was going; I hadn't brought a cell phone. Truth is, I did both those things intentionally. I just wanted time to myself, unattached, unwatched. But as I turned off the main road and started down one of the root sprayed trails, I decided this probably wasn't the smartest thing I'd ever done. But I had noticed that the parking lot at the trail entrance was empty; I'd probably be the only one out there.

So I ran on. A light rain started falling as I pounded down the boardwalk that stretched along part of the trail. Beside the low fronds of palmettos, deer perked their ears at the strumming of my feet and darted for deeper cover. Pine green waters rose on either side of the boardwalk, dispersing into shallow swamp, then wet forest floor.

A mile into the trail, I started to worry that I'd lost my way. I wasn't seeing any signs for the additional paths and the rain was getting heavier so I turned around. As I headed back towards the entrance to the trail and just began thinking about the hot shower I'd take at the bathhouse nestled close to the bus, I saw two young men walking towards me.

"Oh, no," I mumbled to myself.

I am well aware of the fact that those two boys could have been the sweetest, most delightful kids ever born in the great state of Georgia, but I've unfortunately watched too many "Made for TV" movies, too much 11 o'clock news, and to me, this scenario looked bad: a woman running all by herself in the deep woods of a state park, two men with no fishing poles, no running gear, no visible reason to be walking the trails on a rainy afternoon.

As they approached, I sped up my running. I'm a notoriously slow runner, but as I neared them, I got up to a pretty fast clip. They looked like they were in their early twenties, hefty, wearing gym shorts and baggy t-shirts, hats turned cock-eyed; not the nature-loving sort.

I didn't look directly at them as I passed them, just spurted a quick "Hi" and kept my eyes ahead of me, chanting prayers of protection in my head.

"How you doing?" A slow, baritone voice replied as cigarette smoke wafted behind them.

That's when I hit a sprint.

"Oh, God, protect me…" I whispered, tearing up the trail as fast as I could, glancing over my shoulder every hundred feet or so to be sure they didn't turn around. "They're tubby guys," I told myself. "You could outrun them if you needed to." But when I hit the entrance of the trail, I saw their car, the only car, sitting in the parking lot. I couldn't outrun a car.

Constantly looking behind me, I thundered along the ½ mile lonely, forest-lined road, leading back to civilization, a hot flurry of breath and fear and anger. I was blazing mad at myself for being in such a stupid scenario: alone, without a phone, no one knowing my whereabouts. Then, I felt embarrassment that I had stirred a seemingly innocent situation into a full-blown nightmare, a cynic with a dramatic flair. But this highway of emotion finally ended with simple sadness that I live in a world where I had to think about horrific things like abduction, rape, and murder on a peaceful trail run.

Obviously, I made it home unharmed. Half-depressed, I staggered up the bus steps to find the cheerful faces of my husband and two youngest children sitting on the sofa having just finished a rousing reading of Dig, Dig, Digging. *And instantly all the anger, embarrassment, and sadness evaporated, with gratefulness springing up in their stead: thankful that those boys were better citizens than I gave them credit for, thankful for grace filling in for my stupidity, thankful that giggling children still cuddle up in the arms of their father for an afternoon of reading…*

Thankful that the world still has some goodness left in it.

90

> "I travel not to go anywhere, but to go. I travel for travel's
> sake. The great affair is to move."

Robert Louis Stevenson

Saturday night, we cruised north on I-75. We had spent a few
beautiful days at Reed Bingham State Park in Georgia (where
Maile's imaginary mugging took place) and a wonderful afternoon
with friends just outside of Atlanta. By the time we left, it was
growing dark – our destination was a truck stop close to the
Tennessee border. The highway was a sea of red, and rain streaked
the brake lights across the bus's massive windshield in arcs and
splashes. But the traffic charged forward, sweeping us along with it.

In the distance, the lights of Atlanta's skyscrapers rose above the
trees like the center of a newly formed galaxy.

The kids played in the back of the bus, long past their normal
bedtime. Maile sat beside me at the front of the bus, her feet up on
the dash. We talked about how years change people. How life has

made us a little more tired, a little more mature, a touch more cynical, a little less selfish.

Then, we entered the city, the lights rising around us. It's a fascinating feeling, driving through such tall buildings late on a rainy, Saturday night. The lights reflected off the wet highway, battered the windshield. Passing cars glared into my side view mirrors, then flashed past, making disgruntled sounds in the rain. When I opened the small sliding window beside the driver's seat, the smell of wet, hot macadam rushed in to where we sat, filling the bus with an early summer. Lightning flashed. Or was that a streetlight blinking out?

Then, a quiet rustling through the curtain beside me. In the far reaches of my peripheral vision, out at the edge of a different galaxy, 2-year-old Sam had quietly walked to the front, pushed through the curtain that separated us from the back, and sat on the step beside my seat. He looked up through those huge pieces of glass, up through the rain, up at the forty-story office buildings with lights just blinking out.

Like a cricket in the forest looking up at the moon. Was there anything smaller than him in that entire city, looking up at its expanse? For a moment, he seemed like the center of it all.

Then, in a whisper, he said one word:

"Uh-mazing."

"To travel is worth any cost or sacrifice."
Elizabeth Gilbert

One night, I called my mom. Within a few seconds of hearing her voice on the other end of the line, I knew something was wrong.

"Shawn, I have some not-so-good news," she said in a quivery voice reserved for funerals and personal catastrophes.

"What's wrong?" I asked.

"Your aunt has cancer," she said.

It's rather shocking, actually, to discover something like this. It felt like discovering there was a traitor in our midst. I found myself wondering which nearly invisible cells in my own body were planning a revolt. Which tree was going to fall on our bus. I started seeing death behind every oncoming car or hiding in every shadow.

Then, a few weeks later I found out that some very close friends of ours were miscarrying their baby. I didn't know the details. But the sadness was recognizable and reminded me of standing next to Maile at a routine doctor's visit when she was pregnant with our third child. The doctor looked up at us with pursed lips and confused eyebrows.

"I'm really sorry to tell you this," she had said. "But something isn't right." A few weeks later, Maile miscarried. Friends hugged us. We walked around our house quiet and empty.

There is something devastating about hope unattained. The unexpected diagnosis. The bright candle that turns into a smoldering wick. The "something isn't right" speech. Sometimes, just sometimes, it makes me wonder if hope is worth it. Makes me want to live a life where I always expect the worst, keep my hand closed, my eyes on the ground in front of me. Too much looking out at horizons exposes one to the possibility of disappointment.

Then, on a Tuesday evening during our time in Nashville, I went outside to help Maile's brother till his garden. He and I took turns pushing the rototiller around, turning all the old dead grass and hay under the rich brown soil. Then, I raked out the dead stuff to the edges and piled it all into the wheelbarrow. The soil went from looking barren and rather unwilling to expectant. Open.

It takes a lot of turning over to reach that point. A lot of pounding and tearing and grinding of the soil. The rototiller grasped at the

94

ground like giant claws. Our shovels bit into the ground and formed the edge of the garden.

As I worked the soil and the sun dropped behind those Tennessee hills, I thought of my aunt with cancer. My friends losing their baby. They were being tilled. They were being churned up.

But I know them, and I know their hearts. And while it will not diminish the pain they feel now, I marvel at what rich soil they will become.

"Though we travel the world over to find the beautiful, we must carry it with us or we find it not."

Ralph Waldo Emerson

Nashville was beautiful. Nashville was Rivendell. In my mind, I pretended that I would never have to leave. It was a hub of creativity, the source of so many new friendships, the forum for discussions that would float through my mind for months and miles to come. I vowed to come back. I vowed to live there someday.

But eventually, the time came to leave Nashville. Cozy Nashville with its rolling hills and skyscrapers hiding amongst the forest and so many new friends. Our stay there felt much like I imagined base camp would feel to mountain climbers – the last stop, the last stretch of almost-level ground, the last nervous smiles, and all the while the mountain rises up before you, through the clouds.

Just about everywhere we had been up to that point had been some familiar place. But heading west from Nashville, we were destined for Memphis, and I had never been there. Then, we went on to New Orleans for Easter weekend, and I had never been there either. Then west through Texas to California – a million places I had never been.

Occasionally, a foreboding feeling crept up on me, nagged at me from the periphery of my imagination. It lived in dark places previously hollowed out, and eventually abandoned by fear.

This trip is going to change everything, the voice whispers. *You have no idea.*

In some ways, I felt like it already had. I felt like a different person – it proved impossible to meet so many intriguing people, hear so many fascinating stories, see so many different places, without changing.

Yet, I couldn't quite put my finger on it, the exact ways I had been changed. It was such a subtle itch under the skin, an inexplicable ache, growing pains. It was an absence, a tremor.

A sigh.

"No man can be an exile if he remembers that all the world is one city."

C.S. Lewis

We arrived in Memphis where the sky was cobalt blue, the color of an old bruise. The streets glistened, steaming, and even though I couldn't hear the cars through the hotel window, I knew the sound they made on a wet night like that one, their tires shushing everyone.

Friends of ours in Memphis had put us up in one of those long-stay hotel suites, so we basked in the quiet glory of rooms with doors that closed, a real kitchen, and working air conditioning. Cade lay on the fold-out sofa by himself after Sammy had been banished to our bedroom due to the continued performance of acrobatics after bedtime. Lucy was on the recliner, at her insistence. Abra was tucked away in a corner, cuddled up on the sofa cushions that were discarded so the bed could spring into being.

And it was mostly quiet.

During the previous day's drive, somewhere between Nashville and Memphis, the voices had started up again.

"Maybe this was a mistake. You do remember that your current projects end this summer, right? Going on this trip wasn't exactly the most fiscally responsible decision you've ever made."

I had continued driving the bus, staring straight ahead.

"And what about the kids? They could probably use some stability, especially the older two. They are 8 and 7 after all – how are they ever going to make close friends if you keep moving on?"

The narrow road had curled through the Tennessee countryside. Endless acres of forest stretched out in both directions. The bus had crested each hill like a large boat sweeping to the top of a massive wave.

"This whole thing is going to lead to your ruin. Gas prices will skyrocket. You won't finish your current projects in time. You'll go broke. Everyone will use you as the poster child for what goes wrong when someone tries to exist outside of the system. And your glorious, splendiforous failure will put smug smiles on the faces of people who'd like to see such irresponsible behavior nipped in the bud."

I downshifted, let the bus coast up against a lower gear, drifted to the bottom of the swell, then started back up again. I tried to ignore the voices. I tried to focus on the journey.

There had been a valley on 412 somewhere east of Ridgetop, TN, that looked like a river should flow through it. But when the trees parted, and we spanned the bridge, there was no water – only an endless torrent of yellow flowers, winding off in both directions. Yellow as the sun in a child's coloring book.

In another instant, it was gone. Maile had been at the back of the bus, and when she came front I tried to describe it to her, but I couldn't. It was like trying to describe the color yellow to someone who has never seen. Wrinkles of doubt formed in the corners of my mind.

I wondered if perhaps it hadn't been as yellow as I recalled.

The next morning, Maile wasn't feeling so great, and she blogged about the benefits of self-pity.

I'm assuming "allergies" own the tight grip around my lungs at the moment. Every morning, I hack and pound my chest like a 40-year smoker. I'm tired from the beleaguered breathing and broken sleep at night. But I do like my new sexy voice, all raspy and coquettish.

On account of my lingering affair with these allergies, at 10 am this morning (well after my normal "wake-up time"), I found myself lying in the downy blankets of our Memphis hotel bed (an endless thank you to Ron and Nancy for such a luxurious treat). I curled into the fetal position, tight fists pressed against my chest, willing the phlegm to give up and go home, while Shawn sat at the little desk beside the bed studiously working through a writing project.

Out in the living room, the kids flitted between playing matchbox cars, eating strawberries from a white porcelain bowl setting on the coffee table, and watching the premiere of Dora and the Easter Bunny. *From my cocoon on the bed, I could occasionally hear their screams, and I knew our neighbors in rooms 310 and 314 were cursing us.*

I laid there, laboriously coughing, feeling tired and pouty. I wanted my breath back; I wanted our bank account to magically reproduce money well into the thousands; I wanted a governess named Clementine for my children; I wanted all our belongings to be unpacked and organized into a new home in the perfect location for our family's future. To sum it up, I wanted any day but this one.

And you know, sometimes feeling sorry for yourself works. You act like a 2 year-old for 20 minutes or so and bemoan all the things about your life that aren't really that bad (i.e. a bad complexion, a non-existent retirement portfolio, eczema on your feet, poor mothering skills -- I could go on, but I'd just embarrass myself), and God, like the consummate parent that He is, stands there with His arms crossed over His chest taking deep, grace-filled yoga breaths with the faintest hint of amusement sketched on His face.

When my feet pounding, fist clenching, and stuttering sobs subside, He smiles and says:

"Okay, are you done now?"

"Yeah," I sheepishly reply, rather embarrassed by myself.

"Great. Now let's get on with life."

And I get up from the bed, brush my hair, and make lunch.

"Our battered suitcases were piled on the sidewalk again; we had longer ways to go. But no matter, the road is life."

Jack Kerouac

We drove the long straight stretch from Memphis to New Orleans. We crossed the causeways and looked down on the endless swamps with their tiny ramshackle houses accessible only by boat. This sense of isolation joined us on the bus as we arrived at that city, surrounded by so much river and so much marsh and so much emptiness.

We arrived just in time for Easter weekend, and we parked the bus at a campground and went to a small seafood market and bought shrimp and spices and live blue crabs with which we had no idea what to do. We fought the mosquitoes and listened to the deep-throated frogs as they billowed at us from the invisible fringes, and we sat on a picnic table peeling and devouring the best shrimp we'd ever tasted.

I sat at the back of the bus on Friday, Good Friday, and my eyes swam in tears as I soaked up the photos of a memorial service for my dear friends' baby: a willow tree, pink balloons scattered in a blue sky, and a small white box that fit comfortably in one hand.

I think of other friends who will soon accept delivery of a one-week-old baby boy. They will love him and feed him and stay up nights with him until the system decides where to place him: with his biological father or with the parents aching to adopt him. Then, my friends will say good-bye.

One of the most beautiful people I know waits to find out about a certain unexpected spot noticed on a PET scan. Monumental shades, those whites and grays and blacks.

We spend so much time waiting in this world. And there is so much death.

When those who follow Christ break their worldview down into its four most fundamental elements, this is what remains: Incarnation, Death, Resurrection, and Redemption. Three of those find their most powerful roots in this weekend, Easter weekend. A weekend of death, a weekend of resurrection, and a weekend of redemption.

They are monumental, really, these concepts. Life changing. Because who among us has not experienced death? Who among us has never felt that shattering of lost hope? That crumbling of great expectations? That sudden split, like a cracking tooth, when we realize that what we had hoped for will never be realized?

I read a story once about a man who moved to a South American country because he had seen pictures of children living among tall, vaulted piles of stone coffins. The orphans would walk far into this land of death and find old tombs that had broken open, and they would make their home inside of them. This graveyard was one of the few safe places for them in the city because most of those who wanted to take advantage of the orphans were superstitious and would not follow them in to where they lived amongst the ghosts.

When the man arrived in this South American city, he found things exactly as he had heard. The children had created their own city in amongst the graves. Living beside the dead.

There is so much waiting in this world. And so much death.

But don't become too accustomed to foraging among the graves. Don't become numb to the smell that wafts out from the tombs.

Death happens in this life. Dreams shatter. Relationships dissipate. And sometimes it becomes almost comfortable to remain in that broken place because there is a kind of safety in deciding not to hope again. Yet, there is a resurrection waiting to take place in you. A redemption.

A grave is no place to live.

Cade proudly displays two of the massive shrimp we dined on after visiting a seafood market just outside of New Orleans.

"One's destination is never a place, but a new way of seeing things."

Henry Miller

We walked up Tchoupitoulas Street towards the French Quarter in New Orleans. The sky? Blue cotton candy. The breeze? A cool sheet. The streets? Alive and beautiful and carefree.

We walked up Tchoupitoulas Street towards the French Quarter on that day between Good Friday and Easter, and I noticed a man sitting with his back against a vacant building. Crumbling, hollow, condemned: both the man and the building. They seemed to hold each other up. They seemed to weigh each other down.

He nodded at me, right there on Tchoupitoulas Street, his politely parted lips revealing an inexplicable assortment of gold, silver, plaque, and empty spaces. For some reason, the richness of his brown skin immediately made me wonder if he was a grandfather. My youngest daughter, if she would have sat on his lap, would have loved his skin. She would have pulled on it and pinched it and asked him why it was so brown, why it was so freckled. She would have asked him why his teeth were gold or where the missing ones had gone.

But what did he see when he looked at me? Just another person walking by? A young man blessed with money and a nice family?

A rich young ruler?

I stopped, and New Orleans was quiet. My wife looked back over her shoulder. My four children stared at the man, wondered about him, wondered why I stopped. I never used to give money to people without homes, people without jobs, people without hope. "They'll only use it for drugs or alcohol," everyone used to tell me. Then I read something by C.S. Lewis:

Another thing that annoys me is when people say, 'Why did you give that man money? He'll probably go and drink it.' My reply is, 'But if I kept it, I should have probably drunk it.'

I reached into my pocket. A quarter. That's all I had. Twenty-five cents.

"I'm sorry, man," I said, plucking the quarter from my pocket and reaching towards him. "This is all I've got. I wish I had more."

You would have thought I had given him a $100 bill.

"Bless you, brother," he said through a smile verging on tears in a Louie Armstrong voice.

"Bless you, man," I said, turning away, feeling a new weight of sadness, as if I carried that building away with me, on my own back.

Later, we spent $40 at a place called Mother's on an amazing lunch. Jambalaya. Red beans and rice. Shrimp. French Fries. Grits with melted butter. And for the kids, pancakes with butter and syrup. We usually have leftover food when we eat, but it was a late lunch, and we were hungry, and we ate every last bite. And we drank every glass of water at the table.

And it felt so good, being full, and strong, and breathing in the city.

So we walked down Decatur Street in the late afternoon, leaving the French Quarter behind with its beauty and its voodoo and its narrow alleyways. The sun? Glaring and hot. The river? Brown and slow. The clouds? Huge and harmless.

We walked down Decatur Street then turned on to Port of New Orleans Place, a broad sidewalk that flows beside the river. Huge empty stages waited for open air concerts to inhabit them. Docks waited for boats to possess them.

Sitting on a bench was a small woman holding a baby. She held a cardboard sign that read, "My baby and me are homeless."

Probably just a heist to make some money, I thought to myself.

We walked past, and I held my breath the way I always do when I walk past someone like that, waiting for lightning to strike me. Then, another thought.

What the hell is wrong with me?

By then I had six bucks in cash, so I turned around. Again. Always turning. Always stopping. When I walked toward her, her eyes opened wide, as if I was going to beat her for sitting there. Then, when she saw the bills, she jumped – it literally scared her – as if that was even more startling than the fact that I looked at her.

"Thank you, thank you," she just kept saying over and over again. "Thank you, thank you." And I had no reply. Not to her. Not to her child. So I turned my back on her thanks and walked away, shaken.

Along the river, there are those huge binoculars that sit on small pedestals, the ones you have to pay 25 cents to use. The ones through which you can't really see anything.

"Daddy, daddy, we want to look into those things!" my children cried out, their sandals slapping on the concrete as they ran and pushed and vaulted a small wall to get to the magic.

"Awww," Cade complained. "It costs money. It costs 25 cents."

I reached into my pocket; then, I remembered where my last quarter had gone.

Oh, the joy that accompanies empty pockets.

A view of New Orleans, the city that stole our hearts.

"Make voyages. Attempt them. There's nothing else."

Tennessee Williams

We left New Orleans in love with that city. There was a deep craving there, a sense that it was premature to be leaving a place with so many alleys and streets and doorways to explore. It felt like Narnia. It felt like walking into the wardrobe.

We traveled west and eventually crossed the Texas line. The sheer size of the state made us feel as if we were entering another nation. The sky was so large that I realized Texas wasn't its own country – it was its own planet.

After hours on the road, it comes time to look for respite. In Beaumont, TX, we walked into one of those plastic palaces, their AC blasting, their primary colors tearing holes in my retinas. The cool air instantly chilled my skin's thin layer of sweat and grime.

We herded the children to the playground in a separate room and then collapsed into a nearby booth. Maile and I breathed in the cool air and ate slowly, while somewhere off in the distance Cade put Sam in a headlock and both of them screamed and people wondered where those kids' parents were. But we didn't even flinch. We just sat. And breathed. And drank milkshakes.

Eight weeks before that we had pulled away from my parents' house in Paradise, PA. Eight weeks. It felt like years in the past, perhaps even decades. Millennia. Stars had been born, then expanded, and finally collapsed into black holes during the time it had taken for us to drive from Pennsylvania to Florida to Tennessee to Louisiana to Texas.

But we'd reached the halfway point there in that plastic palace. We settled into the long middle stretch, when you begin to question your sanity, your resilience, your ability to make it to the end. Ice cream, which in the beginning was an occasional treat, became the answer to every problem.

The kids removed their shoes in the playground and threw them at strangers. I tapped on the glass like a child at a zoo trying to scare the animals. While I wanted to minimize their savage-like behavior, I also wanted them to burn off as much energy as possible. I gave them a stern look and pointed a menacing finger towards the shoe rack. Their shoulders slumped as if I had told them they were forbidden from having fun for the rest of their lives. They reluctantly returned the weapons to the rack.

I slouched back in the booth. Then, on second thought, I went for a refill of sweet iced tea.

"It's 8:30," I said to Maile after I sat back down. "We should go back to the bus."

"Do we have to?" she asked, sighing, taking another spoonful of milkshake.

"Five more minutes," I said. She groaned. She was worse than the kids.

Later, at 10:07 pm, the inside of our bus was mostly dark, except for the small beams that escaped Cade's bunk where he read long into the night, long after everyone else had fallen asleep. Lucy was in the top bunk, her fan humming. Abra and Sammy slept. Finally.

And no matter how I vowed that I would go to bed early, I simply could not trade those quiet hours for anything. Especially not sleep. So I turned on some music. Maile fell asleep beside me in the bed. I wrote a little. I played Words With Friends. I checked Facebook. I wrote some more.

Then, when I could barely keep my eyelids separated, I put away the computer and read books on my iPhone until I drifted off and nearly dropped the phone on my face. I turned it all off. I gave in. Every possible minute had been squeezed out of that day.

I fell asleep, and I dreamed of wide open spaces.

"The farther you go, however, the harder it is to return. The world has many edges, and it's easy to fall off."

Anderson Cooper

Maile

Guadalupe River State Park, TX:

The kids and I walked down to the Guadalupe River yesterday while Shawn wrote. We heard rumors that there was a nice swimming spot, shallow and not too strong. From the moment Lucy's eyes opened that morning, she begged and whimpered about the river. But there were chores to do and lunch to eat and babies to sleep and school to be done. Each time I said, "After this we will go to the river," I knew in her head she called me a liar. It did seem to take forever to get ourselves in order enough to head out. But eventually everything got checked off the list, and we buckled our shoes, packed a backpack with all the necessities, and pounded our way down the trail.

I hate describing scenery because I really stink at it; my words never paint what my eyes see. But also, I think there's a part of my brain that just switches off

116

when a paragraph of nature imagery begins. Even the greats like Steinbeck could lose me by the second sentence. All that to say, I wish I had the vocabulary that could apply enough color and texture and depth to the description of what we saw as we plodded down the stony path that ended at the river. But I have to try.

On our side of the water, gnarly rooted trees lined the bank occasionally petering out to allow a small stony clearing, perfect for chubby feet to toddle upon and splash into the coolness of a river on an early spring day. On the other side of the bank, rocks laid flat and then stacked themselves one on top of the other like the craziest pile of gray and brown pancakes, teetering high above our heads and the trees around us.

But really, you had to be there.

I normally hate taking my kids swimming. It always seems like such a chore, all the lathering and pulling of spandex and last minute potty emergencies. I do it because my kids love it, and really, I remember being a child myself and absolutely loving to swim more than any other thing on God's green earth. But when we reached that majestic swimming hole yesterday, I thought to myself, "I could do this every day of my life." Talk about a conversion experience.

For about an hour and a half, the kids doggy-paddled and climbed the hunched-over rocks sleeping in the middle of the slowly churning current. Lucy, our resident mermaid, slipped through the water like an oily otter, slithering out of sight for a moment, only to pop up seconds later, shrieking with delight and shivering shoulders.

Eventually, I hiked my skirt up, probably provocatively high to some onlookers, and waded out beside the Littles, ever watchful of the curling water, gathering momentum just beyond the place where they played.

"Look at me, Mama!" Abra shouted over and over again. "Look at me, I'm swimming!" Sure enough, she wasn't. Instead, she floated on her belly and pulled herself along the surface by gripping the stony ground beneath her and slapping her pudgy feet behind her. It most certainly gave the appearance of swimming.

But no matter. She didn't care. She didn't watch Lucy's technique and think, "Really, I should be putting my head in the water, holding my breath, and using smoother, more efficient kicks. Shoot, I really suck at this." Nope, she did what she was good at and was really proud of herself for it.

"Wow, Abra, you're doing a great job!" I gushed.

I could learn a few lessons from my 4-year-old.

Sammy lounges on a rock in the middle of the Guadalupe
River while Cade and Lucy (the two tiny specks on the far
side) go exploring.

"It is always sad to leave a place to which one knows one will never return. Such are the melancholies du voyage: perhaps they are one of the most rewarding things about traveling."

Gustave Flaubert

We enjoyed that peaceful time in the sharp hills just outside San Antonio. The kids swam in the river while Maile sat on the bank, I worked quietly in the back of the bus, and at night, we could smell the wood fires from neighboring campsites. The stars were bright there, so close to the Guadalupe River.

During one of those days, I met up with a client with whom I was writing a book. I'll call him Jack, and he was a retired Navy SEAL. He picked me up in the morning, and we drove into the city to see his friend, a Vietnam Vet. He was insistent that I meet this man, so I went along in spite of my twin phobias of hospital beds and talking to people who are sick.

The VA hospital felt like a morgue for the living. Complete silence. Men in dire conditions sat quietly on scooters or in wheelchairs. They stared at Jack and I as we walked through the front door. I nodded hello to them. Some nodded back. Others did not. I felt very much out of place. For some reason, I also felt very guilty.

"Oh, by the way, we'll need to put on a gown and some gloves before we go in to see Ken," said Jack. "He's got some open sores, nothing infectious, but we should cover up."

I tried to hide my surprise. I thought we were just going in to say hi to a sick veteran, not don full Hazmat suits and enter an area where people's limbs fell off. But it was too late for me to back out, so we stood there in the silent hallway, breaking open plastic bags. Pulling gowns over our heads. Squeaking our way into rubber gloves. I helped Jack slide a glove on to his right hand – after getting shot in the head during a mission and suffering Traumatic Brain Injury, his left hand doesn't work so well for things like that.

We walked up to the open doorway. Jack knocked on the metal frame – cling cling cling – then walked in. I hung back. The man in the hospital bed was not what I had expected.

Once upon a time, Ken had served two tours in Vietnam. Once upon a time, he had been a dog handler and a physical specimen. Once upon a time, he and Jack had done a four-hour swim during Jack's recovery from being shot in the head. I would not have believed any of this, except that these once-upon-a-times hung on

121

his wall in the form of photos. A small, square collage of a life long gone.

Now, just under 500 pounds, he sat in the bed. His chest hung down on to his stomach, which looked immobile. A heart condition had led to an incredible retention of water – left undiagnosed and untreated, his weight had ballooned. A small blanket covered him from the waist down. A large mask covered his face and delivered necessary oxygen. Tubes slid past his nose.

I waited. I expected him to hate me, to stare at me with glowering eyes, wonder why someone would have the indecency to come and look at him, half naked, without permission. To see him at his worst, at his sickest, at his most vulnerable. After all, that's what my response would have been in his situation: lock the door, stay away, don't come near.

But immediately, he smiled and took off the large mask. He sneezed maybe ten times while adjusting to the normal air. We punched knuckles.

"Hi," I said, not knowing what else to say.

"This is Shawn, a friend of mine," Jack said quietly.

"Hi Shawn. How do you know this guy?" he asked. And so started our conversation. And he was normal. He was human. He was kind. I asked him about Vietnam. I asked him about coming back from Vietnam. He was happy to have gone from 492 pounds to 468 pounds that month. He talked and talked about it all, talked as if he never wanted me to leave, talked as if he had been unable to speak his entire life and these were the first fresh words to leave his mouth.

Too soon, we left. He wanted me to come back the next day, or maybe the next week? I explained that we would be on the road, leaving for a new destination. I told him to keep working hard, to keep getting better. We punched knuckles again. I could tell he was disappointed that I wouldn't be back.

Jack and I walked into the hallway. I didn't see another visitor, not in the entire place, just patient after patient who had given his life for this piece of geography I call home. Shattered minds and bodies lay scattered in those quiet hallways, and, besides the staff, no one came to help them gather up the pieces.

Jack and I got into the elevator and rode down to the ground floor. We walked outside and crossed the street. The San Antonio sky felt wider, higher.

Behind us, they prepared to lock the gates for the night.

I was sad to leave him behind. Maile and I both began to sense this feeling of temporariness pervading our travels. Wherever we went, there we were, but it wasn't long before we moved on to somewhere else. Meeting people, connecting with them, and then leaving, became a difficult process. Too many goodbyes.

I awoke this morning and told Shawn I was in a bit of a blue funk. Sometimes it's hard being on the road, being an island in a sense. We go in and out of people's lives every few days, stepping into their day-to-day rhythm, passing their local grocery stores, the bank they deposit at every week, the gym whose membership card is slowly deteriorating away in their wallet. We watch from the outside, looking in, and I see them living what I lived two months ago.

And I miss it in a way.

Don't get me wrong: I'm loving this trip. In fact, sometimes I worry that I will never be able to live any other way than this. I mean really, what will I do when after three days and the newness wears off, I can't lock all my desk drawers, bar the refrigerator door, and sit in "co-pilot" next to Shawn as we rumble down the road to a new, exciting destination? It gets my heart all fluttery just thinking about it.

But I also appreciate the beauty of the routine that I see in the lives of those we visit. Because in routine, you create community. If you eat at the same restaurant every Wednesday morning, you begin to know the people who work there; you establish relationships with the gum-smacking waitress and the bleary-eyed busboy. At the pick-up line at school, you find friendship with the chatty PTA president or the stay-at-home dad who always has the best lunchbox ideas. Or mowing your lawn every Saturday, you find kindred spirits in the neighbors three doors down that now watch your kids during an

124

emergency room visit or bring you fresh tortillas and shredded Mexican beef along with tender hugs after you miscarry a baby you loved and lost too quickly.

Those are the things I miss on this trip: I miss tangible friends; I miss familiar grocery aisles; I miss my mail lady with the badly permed hair and cheery smile.

I guess I miss home.

"Wherever you go, you take yourself with you."
Neil Gaiman

From the outskirts of San Antonio, we made the short jaunt to Austin. The bus glided carefree up and over those hills, and we stared out the windows at such strange scenery.

It was at around this point in the trip that we realized our youngest, Sam, had a huge affinity for watching the landscape roll by. While the other three children played in the back room, Sam would sit at the small booth of a table, rest his elbows up on the narrow ledge that ran along the window, press his face up against the glass, and stare. He has always been by far our most rambunctious child, yet his wild side seemed tamed by the miles of scenery.

One Saturday night in Austin, around midnight, I sat down to reflect on the halfway point of our trip. Two months down, two to go.

The kids slept, and a cool breeze blew in through the bedroom window. Maile was at the table at the front of the bus, writing. I was in the back, in the dark, where I had been stationed until Sam fell asleep – soon he was on his side, wearing only a t-shirt and a diaper, sucking his thumb, taking easy, slow breaths.

Two months. It felt like two years. Or two decades.

We had stood in the midst of a slave graveyard, probing the ground for the missing headstones. I had stared at the stars that night and wondered how such things could ever have been.

We had gotten the bus stuck in a ditch. And then back out again.

My aunt had been diagnosed with breast cancer. And I had felt scared and overwhelmed by her confidence that everything would be okay, and I felt a strong determination to stay positive with her.

We had stood with a crowd of people on the west coast of Florida on an ordinary night and watched the sun drop into the water. And everyone had stood there, their hands still shielding their eyes from a light that was no more, breathless at what they had just seen, frozen as still as if it had been the last sunset.

We had watched storm clouds roll into Memphis like tidal waves.

We had viewed pictures of the memorial service for our friends' not-yet-20-week-old baby. And I had wept at the back of the bus.

We had driven through Louisiana on bridges that went on for miles, bridges that overlooked marshes and dilapidated houses. We had walked the streets of New Orleans and saw pain and beauty. Hope and hopelessness.

We had received a call from my mom that a friend's two-year-old had drowned. Just like that, she was gone. And I think of my own children, and how every second I have with them is grace.

We entered Texas and found it greener than expected, and more beautiful. A good friend took me to the VA hospital and I had spoken with a vet while wearing a hospital gown over my clothes, and we had fist-bumped through latex gloves before I left.

And all along the way we had been blessed by family. Or old friends. Or internet friends we'd never met in real life before. Or complete strangers. Just blessing after blessing after blessing, unexpected, like pulling on your jeans and finding a $100 bill, but better because those blessings couldn't be spent away.

So much death and life in two months. So many things lost and found. So much in the rearview mirror, and so many miles left to go.

"I am grateful for all those dark years, even though in retrospect they seem like a long, bitter prayer that was answered finally."

Marilynne Robinson

Maile

A lot of people have asked me why I wanted to pack all our stuff into a storage unit in Gap, Pennsylvania, corral our four small children onto an old tour bus named Willie, and travel the country for four months with no home or job (for my husband) to come home to.

And here's my stock answer: "Because I've always wanted to travel the country. I just thought it would be interesting and good for the kids' education."

But, really, that's like Miss Nevada saying, "I would wish for world peace" with a cellophane smile held up by double D's in a modest but flattering swimsuit. Sure, she does want peace and I do think all this gallivanting is interesting, but it's such a one-dimensional answer.

129

The truth is: I wanted to take this trip because I flat out NEEDED *it. (And not like you need a vacation to deepen your tan lines and take a break from doing dishes for a while.)*

Last fall, upon the thoughtful recommendation of a dear friend, I began seeing a counselor. During the preceding year I had slowly precipitated into a shadowy cavern, stumbled deep into its damp, musty depths and found a cruel home for my mind there. I went about my physical life in the daylight, feeding my children, teaching their lessons, filling up the grocery cart and smiling politely at the check out clerk.

But as I sat in the parking lot, shifting my car into drive, I felt hopeless. "I can't do this for the next sixty years," I whispered to myself while my childrens' laughter drifted from the back seats.

So I waited, checking off my "to do" list each day, cozying the kids on the couch with a bowl of popcorn and a DVD, then closing my bedroom door and bending over my bed, stifling my sobs with an old down pillow. And I waited.

Then one fall day, my friend posed the right question. "How are you doing?" she asked, not in a flippant, conversation-filling kind of way. No, she asked with her eyes looking directly into mine and her hand holding my elbow. And her question unraveled me.

A month later, after ample dragging of feet and persistent self-declarations that "I can figure this out on my own," I acknowledged my limits and heeded my friend's advice.

130

For my first appointment, I took the back entrance into the office so no one I knew would see me. I hugged the walls like the lead gun in a covert operation. Then I entered the office with a costumed air of cheerfulness; I wanted to give the impression that I was "here for the good of someone else, just getting some solid professional wisdom to pass along to a struggling friend."

I waited nervously in my upholstered chair, nonchalantly flipping through magazines I didn't care about, sneaking eager glances toward the hallway lined with counselors' offices. And then she appeared beside me as I hunched over a recipe for apple doughnuts. I shook her hand, smiled, and strangely felt like a 12 year old meeting her homeroom teacher for the first time; I followed her sheepishly down the hall.

But what transpired in the office down that hallway changed my life.

I began finding hope.
I began seeing goodness.
I began hearing truth.
I began extending forgiveness.
I began feeling love.

But it was just a beginning, the first wobbly steps up the long slippery staircase from my cavern. I felt confident of what I could leave behind in the shadowy place, the past I could set like a statue upon the rocky altars below. But now I needed a journey, a physical odyssey, in order to shed layers, build strength in my legs, and move upwards. I needed this trip to lose myself one night…and find myself the next morning. I needed this trip to sacrifice...and slowly, painfully be born again.

I needed this trip to wrestle, bloodied and grunting in the darkness...to at last receive the blessing of light.

"Every day is a journey filled with twists and turns. Every day, if you smile, you will feel alive, my son."

Santosh Kalwar

For me, Laredo, TX, is where my memories begin. I lived there for a year when I was four. A land of dust. Ants that bite with fire in their mouth. Heat and lizards and trailer parks. Empty swimming pools and a tiny church with cement block walls.

Images of my childhood Texas were much like the memories I have of childhood dreams: stacked haphazardly in the attic of my mind, covered in a fine layer of time, in a spot where, no matter how hard I searched, only the edges were visible.

So when we left New Orleans and headed west towards Texas, I had certain expectations of what I would see. I think dust was the main one followed closely by shimmering waves of heat, armadillos, and vultures. Yet, the further west we drove in

Louisiana, the more confused I became because, well, the landscape was still unexpectedly green.

Perhaps it will happen at the Texas border, I reasoned. Perhaps the sign "Welcome to Texas" will be a small part of a great line that stretches as far as I can see to the north and south, a line separating green Louisiana from a dusty brown Texas.

But it didn't happen. There was no such divide. In fact, the deeper into Texas we drove, the more beautiful it became. Oaks and Mesquite covered the rolling landscape, growing alongside rocks and cacti. The trees were lower, like servants cowering from the sun, but there was something majestic in the harshness, something tantalizing in amongst the shade. I wanted to know more about those trees.

Turns out, Mesquite trees thrive in Texas for a few interesting reasons: they have what's called a tap root, some of which have reached 190 feet under the ground; they can regrow from six inches underground if the trunk is destroyed; and even a piece of Mesquite root placed in the soil can regenerate into a new tree.

There is something to be said for deep roots. There is something to be said for pushing up from under the ground.

There is something to be said for being broken and split and pulled from the earth, yet maintaining a determination to grow again.

**"Set out from any point. They are all alike. They all lead to a
point of departure."**

Antonio Porchia

Maile

April 15ᵗʰ, 2012- Austin, TX

*We had such a great day with Shawn's Uncle Sam today. First, we went to the
Inner Space Caverns near Round Rock. Wow, how beautiful and strange. The
Bigs loved it; the Littles tolerated it. Then, we had a bite of lunch at Chipotle
before heading to the playscape display over at Sam's office. When we pulled
into the parking lot, I heard every decibel of gasping: "Wow!" "Are we allowed
to play on these?" "Are these all his?" A tangible heaven to four road-weary
kids.*

*And so the play began. Like a child's version of Supermarket Sweep, they ran
helter-skelter around the grounds, frantically scaling the small climbing walls,
giving every steering wheel they passed a wild spin; then, off they ran to the next*

135

wooden playhouse or vacant swing. Honestly, they didn't stay on one playset for more than 30 seconds; they were simply determined to enjoy a little bit of each thing rather than gorge themselves on one slide or swing, missing out on all the others around them. What a strange and hilarious spectacle to watch.

About 10 minutes into the cacophony of play, Shawn decided to reel things in a bit by starting a game of Hide and Seek. I meandered around, helping the Littles find less obvious hiding places (sitting on a swing kind of took away the mystery of Hide and Seek), and cheering for the Bigs as they attempted to outrun their galloping, screeching father.

Then, two rounds later, Shawn's "Smucker-ness" came out.

Now, if you know anything about the Smuckers, you know they love competition and they love games. Even now, as Shawn's aunts and uncles are in their fifties and sixties, they don't bat an eye at a hot and heavy game of volleyball, complete with diving to the floor for the ball or smashing it over the net. They're a feisty bunch.

That said, Shawn couldn't bear that his Uncle Sam and I were just refereeing this game of Hide and Seek; he wanted us in on it. Of course, Sam was just waiting for the invitation. Like a spry 10-year old, he jogged off to hide in small shed nestled on the outskirts of the playsets. The Bigs and Littles nervously giggled as they fluttered from potential hiding spots, never sure where to settle. Shawn counted on, yet, there I stood, the battle inside me raging.

136

Sometimes, I think I wear this "mother" role a little too tightly. Occasionally, deep inside, I feel the desire to act childish once again: jump eagerly into a game of hide and seek, tear out a Strawberry Shortcake coloring page and bring it to life with a fistful of crayons, or twirl around in the cool rain with no regard for the mud on my shoes or my sopping t-shirt.

But when those desires whisper in my mind, "Mother-talk" kicks in: "Now, Maile, you really shouldn't do that. You're a mom now. If you aren't behaving responsibly, who will? There always needs to be someone in charge, an adult on the scene. That's your job now." So I suppress the desire and just be "Mama."

Except today. By the time Shawn's counting reached to fifty, I was snuggled into one of the round cylinders on the train playset, breathless with anticipation, the sweet nervousness of childhood pounding in my chest. And when Shawn trickled away from base looking for prey, I darted for safety, laughing like my 7-year old, light on my feet, and wonderfully weightless in my heart.

My Uncle Sam in Texas (who we affectionately refer to as
Uncle Chub). His playsets and gazebos were a welcome
energy drain for the kids. His texts and encouragement
during the trip often brought tears to our eyes.

> **"The seeker embarks on a journey to find what he wants and discovers, along the way, what he needs."**
>
> **Wally Lamb**

It's a smaller world now. We drive 10,000 miles in four months. We devour states the way my childhood self inhaled birthday cake. We breathe in the miles and exhale them before ever really catching their scent, before ever really tasting the dust. The grit of every city coats our teeth, but we clean it from our mouths with the water of movement, of speed, of change.

The road we followed north from Ft. Worth to Tulsa stretched out in front of us. I wondered about the distance – we crossed that expanse in hours. Felt like minutes. Somehow it seemed like we were cheating, skipping through such demanding terrain without a second thought. Before the land was settled, it would have taken days. Weeks.

Or perhaps a lifetime. Perhaps the distance seemed so great back then that most people never left. Most people stayed. It wasn't only their hometown – it was their world, their galaxy, their universe. Nothing existed outside of those rolling hills, the endless miles of trees, the sky that threatened to engulf everything.

Just a few nights ago, before this drive north, Maile and I had sat on the front porch with a good friend in Fort Worth, TX, talking about books and children and moving. We drank red wine. Her neighbor saw us and came over, pulled up a chair. The neighborhood kids ran through the falling dusk, playing tag in a whirling cloud around us, like moths flitting around a porch light.

Sam and Abra ran senseless through the yard – they did not understand the rules. They simply ran because everyone else ran. Sam raised his hand in defiance, shouted a barbarian shout, took a swing at passing kids with a foam sword. Abra laughed and laughed, even as her eyes swelled with allergies. Then, she came over and leaned her head on my leg, and I cleaned her eyes gently with a wet paper towel.

Lucy, quiet Lucy, ducked her chin down towards her sternum and took six brave steps towards the tree that was base. A few of the girls explained the rules in matter-of-fact tones to her, as if Lucy was no stranger to them. She leaned towards the tree, put her hand on that holy icon, her deliverance.

I found Cade in the bedroom playing with marbles. He needed some coaxing, but soon, he galloped through the Ft. Worth night with the other kids, shouting to his new-found friends.

And us four adults, we drank in the night – the shouting, the shadows – long after our glasses were empty.

It's a smaller world now. A world where children from Pennsylvania can play hide-and-seek in Austin one day, then freeze tag in Dallas the next, then soccer in a Tulsa field a few days later. A world where I can give my last quarter to a man in New Orleans, then a few days later have my life changed by a Vietnam Vet struggling in a hospital bed in San Antonio.

We devoured the states as we passed through them. We gorged ourselves on miles traveled. But I hope I never take these stories for granted, the stories of real life people. The woman and her child begging in the French Quarter. The voodoo man with animal bones tied around his neck. The patient I could not touch with bare skin.

I never want to wash the memory of them away.

"The way through the world
Is more difficult to find than the way beyond it."

Wallace Stevens

Friday morning, 2am, and a thunderous rain pounded on the roof of our bus. Flashes of lightning dashed inside to where we slept, and, quickly following after, thunder split my children's dreams.

Friday morning, 2am, and Lucy wriggled her way into our bed with the irrefutable password. "I'm scared," she whispered, curling up under the quilt with her mother, right up against her stomach, as if wiggling her way back into the womb. Sammy wasn't far behind – he took my place in the bed, relegating me to Lucy's bunk (I actually love sleeping in those tiny bunks).

Friday morning, 2am, and I lay in the bunk, listening to the storm. Sometimes, I worried about invisible things: that my writing would never reach the heights I dreamed; that I would hurt those closest

142

to me with one bad decision; that I would reach a later age and want a redo on the choice I made to live an adventurous life.

These were the thoughts that came in the middle of storms. The sentences in my brain were frantic, like the rain. The sentences in my brain were flavored by the lightning, punctuated by the thunder.

Friday morning, 11am, I sat in a coffee shop and wrote the stories about which I dreamed. I drank a mocha, and I read the creativity of my friends, and I thought about how that crazy family of mine was in Tulsa, visiting the wonderful Luitwielers, and how next week we would be in Amarillo, and, the next, Pasadena.

Life was almost always good when I rested in the here. The now. The frightful days that circled in my mind during a late-night thunderstorm rarely saw the light of reality. The cool mornings after storms gave me hope, when the gray sky apologized sheepishly for all the fuss it had made the night before. I drank my coffee and was reminded that autumn would circle around again. Cool mornings would come after the summer, mornings that required quilts and sweaters.

The heat of summer would not last forever.

Hope would circle around again.

"A journey of observation must leave as much as possible to chance. Random movement is the best plan for maximum observation."

Tahir Shah

Driving west from Tulsa to Amarillo on a bright afternoon, you could measure the passing of time by the distance the sun traveled down the bus's massive windshield. Every hour or so I pulled on the string that lowered the screen that shaded my eyes from the glare. By about 7:00 pm, the screen was as low as it would go, and the sun had fallen beneath it, blinding.

Huge gashes tore through the land in that part of the country: deep gorges formed by the tiniest creeks, or flat expanses of bare ground turned over by a farmer. The earth was red there, where the green grass was pulled back or split. Kind of like wounds, or cuts, but not the smooth kind made by scalpels – those were rough injuries.

I thought about those who lived in that part of the country long ago, the ones whose land we stole. I thought of how their life had

144

spilled into the earth. The water standing in the ponds took on the red color of the soil, looked like pools of clay-colored blood.

I couldn't remember ever being able to see so far. The height of the sky seemed the same, but out at the horizon, around the edges, the sky looked like someone had stretched it. My eyes were telescopes. I could see small specks of cattle a thousand miles away. Huge power lines rose no higher than the width of my little finger.

It was easy to feel small out there, where I could drive a hundred miles without seeing a house. It was easy to feel like the whole world had expanded, and my existence had shrunk. And it wasn't such a bad feeling. There is so much pressure on us to feel big, to feel important, that the lessening of this actually provides relief.

A dirt road ran parallel with the highway, and a teenager driving an old Chevy pickup tried to keep up with the highway traffic. Dust billowed out behind his bald, anxious tires like the years of my youth: tempestuous and exciting and then settling, diffusing. He surged ahead. Later on, we passed him. He had stopped at a crossroad and was deciding which way to go.

The sun dropped below the horizon just as we entered Amarillo, and the sunless sky felt cool against my eyes. We pulled into a large parking lot a day earlier than expected. Maile popped popcorn for the kids, and the smell of it filled the bus. We put in a movie. They perched on the couch, all four of them in a row like birds on a wire, cramming popcorn into their mouths.

It was a late night in Amarillo. The old man slept loudly beneath the bus.

Maile

Yesterday, Shawn and I drove along the five hours of road from Oklahoma City to Amarillo. The terrain kept changing itself, first flat and endless, then undulating and pockmarked with small canyons and gorges. And then, in what seemed a quick breath, the land leveled out once again, dotted with cattle and tattered ranch houses.

"I think I could like owning a ranch," Shawn said beside me, double-fisting the wheel of the bus while gazing at the sprawling fields.

"Yeah," I replied, kind of breathy, my eyes still scanning the green and brown prairie outside my window. The land mesmerized me.

I don't know these people who populate these dusty, abandoned towns along route 40 heading west to Amarillo. From the billboards, I know they don't have a McDonalds within 70 miles of their front door. I know that the indigo sky at 8:45 in the evening makes you feel like there is nothing on earth between you and heaven. I know that men in cowboy hats really do drive rusty pick-ups down dirt roads at 80 mph, stirring up dust clouds that look perfectly Hollywood.

And I know that landscape broke my heart and mended it at the same time. I wanted it so badly, to roll it up like a scroll, slide it into an empty wine bottle,

146

and cork it just to savor again 20 years from now. But it went on for miles, far too big to shake out like a sheet and fold away.

That's what I loved about it: I breathe easier in all that space.

Tonight, Sammy has made it abundantly clear that sleep will not come quickly. He fusses and squirms, reaching into his tiny little gut and forging these tortured cries for "drink" and "Mama."

So I sit beside him, and he dangles his pudgy fingers close to my knee. He wants me close enough that he can smell the garlic from dinner in my clothes and the sweatiness of spending hours in the Amarillo cool breeze and hot sun. And he wants to touch: he wants me to pet the palm of his hand and rub his satiny soft forearms.

"Scratch my back," he whispers, reaching his short stubby arm behind him, trying to give me a quick lesson in proper technique. So I lightly skim my sandpaper fingers across his tiny back, and he giggles. Then, I lay my palm down flat, moving rhythmically across his baby round ribs undulating beneath his peachy skin. The crying, the rustling, the whimpering subside; his eyelids bob towards sleep.

And he breathes easier with no space at all.

Cade and Lucy cooling off while on a hike with Maile through the Palo Duro Canyon just outside Amarillo, Texas.

"Just when you think you've hit rock bottom, someone will hand you a shovel."

Jill Shalvis

I suppose everyone has a particular way of dealing with rock bottom. Some folks eat a pint of Ben and Jerry's "Chocolate Therapy." Others watch 6 seasons of *Lost*, 10 episodes at a shot for a week or two, just to escape.

For me? I always know when I've hit rock bottom because I go to Monster.com and start looking for "real" jobs. This never helps because I quickly realize how unemployable I am. When you put writing into a job search, mostly what comes up are notices for insurance sales or telemarketing. Or paid ads for MFA programs.

My breathing slows, and I start to consider how embarrassing it will be to move back in with my parents. I consider all of the more nefarious ways I could generate income, such as selling my organs on the black market or off-loading bodily fluids for cash.

Then, there was the day when the Amarillo sky was low and gray, the clouds providing welcome relief from a sun that torched us the day before with high temperatures around 99 degrees. And the wind. There was always the wind. The trees bent towards the north, the pale undersides of their leaves glaring silver.

I sat outside the Starbucks in our gray minivan and considered the fact that my current projects end in a few months, and I have no guaranteed income beyond that. I considered the cost of diesel. The cost of four children going to college. And I opened up Monster.com.

On the Sunday morning that we left Tulsa, almost a week before, it had been cool and windy. I had gone outside to get the bus ready for departure. This involved, among other things, emptying the waste tank and filling the fresh water. I had sat down on the ground beside the hose, turned it on, and then waited.

As I had sat there, I realized that it had been quite some time since I had just sat quietly. Not writing. Not driving. Not messing around on my phone. Just sitting, available, listening to the muse or to God or to the wind.

Strange. Tangled up knots inside of me had started to loosen. I sensed God there. Maybe it was the quiet, or the cold, or the sense of adventure that always fills me before we embark on the next leg of our journey. But it had been a spiritual experience, sitting quietly, emptying the bus's waste tank. Filling the fresh water.

Back to Amarillo and the huge puddles that remained after the hail storm that had passed through earlier in the day. The sun set. I arrived back at the bus and sat down to write. I listened to The National's song "About Today." The wind pounded the bus, swaying it back and forth. Cade came out to ask if we would tip over. I assured him we would not. Inside, I wondered.

I felt scattered on that night (can you tell by the ridiculous jumps in the writing?). I felt uncertain. Yet there was a simple assurance in the quiet. A sense of peace in the wind. It's the same peace I had felt while sitting outside the bus in Tulsa a week before. The kind of peace that wraps around you, even when you're emptying the waste tank.

I thought of the poet Billy Collins' words,

What scene would I want to be enveloped in
more than this one

And I realized there wasn't one.

Our first glimpse of snow-capped mountains, somewhere in northern New Mexico.

"Getting lost is just another way of saying 'going exploring.'"

Justina Chen Headley

It was an epic trek, that drive from Amarillo towards the Grand Canyon. Our bus took us through deserts and over mountains. We meandered slowly through cities and flew past the rocky outcroppings of dreams. For the first time, we were introduced to the Southwest, and it was beautiful and foreign and tantalizing.

We spent the first night in a Walmart parking lot somewhere around Carson National Park in New Mexico after a mind-numbing drive during which we saw the most beautiful scenery I have ever seen. Of course, the only reason we saw what we saw was because we were lost, which in itself is an endorsement for letting yourself lose your way every once in a while.

The morning after that long drive, we made our way to Four Corners, the spot on the planet that joins Utah, New Mexico, Arizona and Colorado. We pulled off a staged photo and made jokes about the rotten kinds of parents who leave their children in four states. We went back up out to the bus and sat there for a moment, exhausted by the sheer number of miles, the inexplicable number of new things we had seen.

I had never expected Arizona to be so cold in April, but a cool desert breeze dashed along the rocks and the dirt and the plateaus, felt more like a late-fall morning in Pennsylvania. The market surrounding the Four Corners monument had only begun to wake up. Vendors pulled up in their pick-up trucks, held steaming cups of coffee, chatted with one another, and shrugged their shoulders at the slow start to the day.

Then, hungry, I got out of the bus and meandered up to one of the small food shacks. It was nothing more than a metal concession trailer with a plywood room somehow fastened alongside. Inside, a makeshift counter ran along the walls where people could stand and eat. Country music scratched out from an old portable radio.

I ducked into the small shelter and put my arms up on the high counter, nearly chin height. Two iron skillets waited on unlit gas burners. A woman emerged from the corner of the aged, clean kitchen. Her black hair reminded me of the dark night we had driven through to get there. She offered me a reserved smile, a small row of the whitest teeth shining through her plump, tan skin. It was obvious that her ancestors were the original people of this immense land.

"What can I get you?" she asked quietly. No pretense. No sappy customer service. Simply a question that needed answering.

"I'd like an order of fried bread with powdered sugar," I said.

"It will be just a few minutes," she replied, turning her back.

Waiting for my order (the sign declared it a Native American specialty), I wandered back out into the hot sun, felt the cold breeze, and stared out into a foreign landscape. I might as well have strayed on to another planet.

The ground was formed out of pebbles, and dust. These created a soil that supported small, hearty shrubs and larger rocks, which in turn held up mesas and plateaus. This order of things remained uninterrupted to the horizon. To the south, a massive mountain. Far to the east, barely visible, snow-capped peaks.

I saw only one house in all of those tens of thousand of acres, and it slept in a deep valley created by steep-edged mounds of rock and earth. It was a mobile home, and it held tightly to a fence, five cars, and a few ramshackle outbuildings. That's it. One house by itself for as far as I could see.

There is something about the west that immediately grabbed on to my heart. The open, rugged terrain awakened something in me, something adventurous and hopeful. The physical emptiness left room for a spirituality that filled the wind and the sky. It was a beautiful, mystical, foreboding place.

The kind of place where anything could happen.

I stepped back into the food shack. She brought my fried bread, and I paid her, and that was it. But I wanted to say something. I wanted to say, "I know what you have given up." I wanted to say, "I would be on your side, if it happened again." But I was too tired, or too intimidated, and besides, none of it was probably true anyway, so I walked back to the bus with a piece of fried dough covered in powdered sugar.

We drove through Navajo country all day. The few small towns we encountered were random scatterings of mobile homes. Each surrounded by a fence. Piles of tires. Cars on blocks. Chained dogs sleeping in the dust.

We passed a hitchhiker once. 200 years ago he would have been a Brave on a beautiful horse, proud and stern. But in this world, and in this time, he didn't even raise his thumb to us. Just leaned back against the road sign and crossed his legs, his tattered clothes grabbing on to the red dirt. He reached up and licked the tip of his thumb, as if preparing to separate two thin sheets of paper. Our eyes met as the bus passed.

Maile took a picture of a rocky outcropping, the kind you get used to seeing while driving through that part of the country. It came up

156

out of the ground like the stump of some massive tree destroyed long ago or a pillar holding up the temple that is this earth.

In the foreground of the stone monument sat yet another trailer. A few old cars. The present reality of poverty was still overshadowed by the reminder of what should have been.

Only extremely irresponsible parents leave their four children in four different states. Cade, Sam, Abra and Lucy pose at Four Corners.

"The wonders of the Grand Canyon cannot be adequately represented in symbols of speech, nor by speech itself. The resources of the graphic art are taxed beyond their powers in attempting to portray its features."

John Wesley Powell

One question surfaced throughout the trip, usually voiced by Cade or Lucy:

"Is the Grand Canyon bigger than that?"

When we drove over bridges a few hundred feet above the water:

"Is the Grand Canyon bigger than that?"

When they swam in a river with a huge rock face on the opposite bank:

"Is the Grand Canyon bigger than that?"

When Maile took them to the Palo Duro Canyon in Amarillo:

159

"Is the Grand Canyon bigger than that?"

And our answer was always the same:

"Oh, yes. Much bigger."

So it was with nearly held breath that we approached the southern rim of the Grand Canyon. Up up up the bus toiled, from the desert floor and into the rocky landscape where evergreens held up the wide sky. The mountain dropped off to our right, just past the guardrail, down into the beginnings of the canyon.

"Is the Grand Canyon bigger than that?"

"Oh, yes. Much bigger than that."

Then, we crept away from the edge, the road going deeper into the forest. We paid to enter the park, forged ahead. Maile sat in the passenger seat, and the four kids peered off to the right, through the trees, desperate for their first glimpse of this immense thing we had been discussing for the last two months.

Then, there it was.

It came out of nowhere: the trees fell away, and there, just under the edge of the bus, the unfathomable drop down the rocky gorges of the Grand Canyon.

Maile's face froze, her eyes unblinking. Sam and Abra pressed their noses up against the glass. Cade turned white.

"Oh......my......" he said, his voice trailed by slow breathing.

But Lucy, her response topped them all. She turned to Maile and I, worry etched in every perfect pore of her 7-year-old face.

"We'd better keep a close eye on Sammy," she said earnestly.

For three days, we wandered that part of the country that seems to border the edge of the world (and we did have to keep a close eye on Sammy). We listened to park rangers explain the history of the Grand Canyon, its discovery, its preservation. We watched in horror as high school kids climbed out beyond the chain link fences and walked gingerly along the Canyon's edge. We stared down into its depths, always trying to locate that thin thread of a river that made its home so entrenched.

It felt like we had seen something important, something that wouldn't vanish from our memories. Beauty contains such depth, the power to wear us down, the ability to reach previously unexplored parts of us.

The kids get their first glimpse of the Grand Canyon from outside of the bus. The black and white photo does the canyon a huge disservice.

"One of the great things about travel is that you find out how many good, kind people there are."

Edith Wharton

I made some very expensive transactions on this trip. Nearly everywhere we went, I gained something, and I left something behind.

In Virginia, in a small town named Bremo Bluff, we gained a kind friend who treated my kids like they were his grandchildren. He built a small fire under that southern night sky for marshmallow roasting. And I left a piece of myself on that farm while struggling to comprehend a world where slaves used to look up at those same stars.

In New Orleans, we wandered the streets in the French Quarter, taking everything in, and I was left wondering about a homeless man sitting on a step when all I had to give him was a quarter.

In Tulsa, our friends welcomed us into their regular life, and it was good. We ate dinner in their house and went to soccer games, and for a few days we weren't road warriors, just residents of a middle American city.

In northern New Mexico, we got lost around Carson National Park. At one point, the road scaled the side of a cliff – glancing back, we saw a small, green valley hidden among the red rocks. A winding stream, lined with trees, disappeared into a canyon etched in the side of the mountain. If I could have stayed there, I would have. I can still see that perfect valley in my mind.

From New Mexico into Arizona, I was left speechless by the beauty of the landscape. And I ached as I saw the poor living conditions of the Native Americans who used to roam freely under that massive sky.

All over the country, we made friends, and then we left them behind.

These are the transactions that occur when you live a life of faith: you receive beauty and unexpected grace, but sometimes in exchange you lose everyday comforts. You lose a sense of ownership. Some things make less sense. Some things take on added meaning.

During the early days of our trip, my sister and brother-in-law had received a call from child services. Would they be interested in providing cradle care for a child who's parentage was uncertain? The father had decided to claim parental rights but had a process to go through. The adoptive parents were hesitant to take in the baby if the father was going to get involved.

So my sister and brother-in-law took the little one in. They fed him every three hours. They got up with him in the night. They changed his diapers.

But even more importantly, they invested huge pieces of themselves into his young life, not knowing how long he could stay with them. Today? This week? Longer?

This is the walk of faith: giving without thought of what will be gained. Receiving beauty and unexpected grace in the midst of so much potential heartache. So much potential love.

Before you, two paths. One of comfort and predictability. The other? Faith and adventure.

Today we drove north to San Francisco, and then the monumental turning:

East.

"Our native soil draws all of us, by I know not what sweetness, and never allows us to forget."

Ovid

Then, one of those melancholy nights that come three-fourths of the way through a trip, when you're sad that so much of the trip is behind you, and sad that you still have so far to go before getting home.

The kids played at the back of the bus, Sammy's little shout punctuating their pretend world. Maile sat beside me, slowly eating an ice cream bar. Outside, the sun dropped until its light hit that particular angle where everything was split into light sides and dark sides. Even the lowest things leave long shadows.

One of my favorite albums started playing: Druthers' *Lots and None At All*, and suddenly the strangest thing: I felt homesick. For the first time on that crazy trip, a small ache for familiar things, a longing for routine. I was blindsided by a desire for the mundane.

166

I'd be dishonest if I didn't admit to some occasional anxiety regarding the future. Current projects were coming to an end, and there wasn't a lot of writing work on the horizon for me, at least none that I could see.

Yet, I knew that was where we were supposed to be. Traveling the country. Too many things had led us to that place. We had had too many awesome experiences. I had met too many inspiring people. No matter what direction the road ended up taking, it had been too good to second-guess.

It was E.L. Doctorow's whole business with the headlights. You know, how driving at night you can never see beyond your headlights, but you can make the whole trip that way.

The kids moved to the table and started writing out postcards to some of their friends. We hadn't been so good about helping them stay in touch – not for their lack of writing. But most of the pieces of correspondence they did write ended up lost somewhere in the bus. I found a small pile of letters the other day. They had fallen down beside the desk.

Sometimes prayers feel that way don't they? Like misplaced correspondence. Like well-crafted words, letters we spend so much time creating, yet messages that in the end don't quite end up in front of the person for whom they were intended.

But there was hope, too, more hope than I had ever felt before. An exciting sense of expectation: a strange sense that anything could happen.

"I feel as if I had opened a book and found roses of yesterday sweet and fragrant, between its leaves."

L.M. Montgomery

Maile

Shawn and I parked the bus at a campground just North of San Francisco. I came here a couple of times as a child with my family, to see the sights and visit my grandfather who lived in Sacramento. In the cob-webbed cupboards of my mind, I've stored images of weaving down Lombard St. in a stuffy rental car; gazing, frightened and intrigued, at the fuzzy image of Alcatraz through the cheap lenses of pre-pay, mounted binoculars; and the towering majesty of centuries-old Redwoods standing as sentries along the rocky streams of Muir Woods.

But each memory is merely a silhouette, a deep outline but no details in the middle, until one moment stands out full and weighty with color, texture, and emotion.

That moment portrays a long-haired child bending over a thorny, blossom-bursting yellow rose bush beside her grandfather. He is handsome, white hair reflecting off skin tanned by the suns of Hawaii and California over 60 plus years. His smile dazzles, roping my young heart like he lassoed so many others throughout the years (he left a trail of broken, wandering hearts behind him).

But not mine.

With the steady hand of a skilled gardener, he snips the stem of a budding flower at a precise angle. And he hands it to me. Placing my fingers to offset the thorns, I take it from him and tears trickle down my cheeks. We are leaving, and I don't want to say good-bye.

When we got back to Ohio, when the petals began to wilt at their edges and hunch their shoulders, my mom pulled out the creaky ironing board from the laundry room, placed my tired rose upon it and entombed it between two sheets of wax paper. I kept it in my memory box, and every month or so, teetering on an old wooden chair, I'd pull it down from my closet shelf and finger its pressed profile.

Years later, my mom called me to tell me that my grandfather was dying. She asked me to fly out to Ohio to meet up with her and my dad, then fly on to Sacramento to say farewell. But I couldn't go. I wouldn't go. I feigned some important obligation I simply couldn't break. But really, I was afraid: afraid of flying, afraid of death, afraid of sadness, afraid that the frail old man lying in a bed dying of emphysema would erase what I remembered of him as a child.

But here I am now, driving the same highways he once did and gazing upon landscapes that provided the backdrop for his later years. And I wish I had a do-over. I wish I had folded fear into my bedside drawer, boarded that plane, and said a proper "good-bye" to my grandfather.

But I didn't.

A couple days ago, I started out for a jog, turning out of our RV park and down a smooth sidewalk lining dated little houses along a quiet street. As my gaze swung to my left, I saw an elevated flower bed just ahead of me, lined with rose bushes, each a different color: red, orange, pink…and yellow.

I smiled, tears quivering along the rims of my eyes, and I thought:

I'm not afraid anymore.

When we return from our trip in about 6 weeks and when we have a home again with perhaps a little square of green and brown earth, I think I'll bend over a hole dug with the pink and blue spades of my four children. And I'll plant a bush that will bloom with yellow roses.

"Maybe everyone can live beyond what they're capable of."

Markus Zusak

The Redwood trees stood massive and solemn, some close to 300 feet tall, some over 500 years old. I felt small and insignificant under their kind shadows. Like an ant. Or a long-forgotten worry.

These very same trees stood while the first Europeans docked their ships and slid small boats up on to the sand of East Coast beaches. They grew slowly, ring outside of ring, oblivious to the world tightening around them.

Then, a voice no explorer had ever heard. My daughter Abra.

"I have to go potty!" Abra exclaimed somewhere deep in the Redwood forest.

We had left the last "potty" about a mile behind us. I looked at Mai and shrugged.

172

"I'll take her back if you can herd these three," I suggested, motioning towards the other kids.

So Abra and I walked back the way we had come. She occasionally darted ahead to show how fast she could run, her long blond hair waving back at me. Just as quickly she stopped, her butterfly-like attention grabbing fully on to anything that interested her.

"The letter 'A'!"

"Look at that little bird!"

"I want to kiss that lady!"

Almost at the restrooms, she ran over to one of those small podiums with some information about an interesting something or other.

"I want to read this," she said.

"What about the potty?" I asked.

"No! I want to read this!"

So I lifted her up so she could see the words (she couldn't read yet, but she pretended that she could – usually her pretend reading was way more interesting than what the words actually said). The display explained the strange grove of trees right in front of us. Trees I would have missed if she hadn't stopped me.

A huge grove of six or seven Redwoods gathered, each three to five feet in diameter. They had grown in an almost perfect ring. In their midst stood the charred remains of an old Redwood. Before some ancient fire, it had reached up higher than a fifteen-story building. Now, it was barely fifteen feet tall. The outside of it was black, the hollow inside crumbling.

The old blackened Redwood must have died in a forest fire. But its roots had survived, and out of that underground life sprang the circular grove of Redwoods in front of us. The fire could only kill what was above ground, and after a time, the new trees grew up out of the old roots.

I so badly want my here-and-now to be the thing that survives. I work so hard to protect it, to nourish it, to save it from the fire.

But what if my "today" must die in order for such prolific life to rise? What if the destruction of this current beauty must take place so that the root of something even more glorious can push up new shoots through the darkness?

Shawn and the kids pose in front of a Redwood tree.

"Not all those who wander are lost."

– J. R. R. Tolkien

It was Sunday night, and I was in the bed at the back of the bus. It was peaceful there: the three oldest kids were in their bunks with the occasional complaint about an early bedtime; Maile wrote at the front of the bus; and Sam had just crawled into bed beside me moments before, sucking his thumb and turning his blanket around and around and around, looking for the corner where the label sticks out.

The following day, a Monday, represented a rather momentous day for us: for the first time in three months and over 5,000 miles, we would head east. Our trip had begun back in February when we headed south down the east coast, meandered through the southeast in March, drove west through Oklahoma and Texas in April, then cruised north up the California coast.

176

But on Monday we would head east.

So many feelings surfaced as I considered heading east: relief that the trip was almost over; dread that the trip was almost over; excitement to see what the next few months would hold; fear about what the next few months would hold. Heading east meant returning to friends and family, a community that we missed and the place I had grown up. All good.

But the adventure, in its messiness and its fast pace and its immediacy, sometimes allowed me to overlook the pressing sorts of big picture issues I'd rather not think about. Such as the fact that my current projects ended in June. Such as the fact that at that point we did not have a home of our own to go back to. Such as the fact that our travel expenditures had exceeded our budget by a good bit (thanks, diesel prices). Returning home from such an adventure would mean laying aside the exciting for the practical, the unexpected for the everyday.

But I concluded that this, also, was a good thing. The adventure, while it lasted, had broken many areas of my life down to their most basic elements, then allowed me the space and time to build those areas back up. My marriage. Being a dad. Writing. Mile by mile, I reconstructed myself.

So we would head east. It was hard to believe. There wasn't a whole lot that I would have been able to tell you about what my life would look like in a month's time. Where we'd live. What I'd be doing for a living. But as I wrote, I realized that whatever happened would simply be a continuation of this grand adventure, and I gradually became okay with that.

Better than okay – I was eager for it. I was eager to live life. Just about anything seemed possible at that point. I decided to let that fill me with a sense of anticipation, not a sense of worry.

We watched the sun set into the Pacific from a solitary bench
we found on a California hillside. Lucy seems particularly
pleased, but she should be, because it was cold and there was
only one sleeping bag and she was in the middle.

"When we get out of the glass bottle of our ego and when we escape like the squirrels in the cage of our personality and get into the forest again, we shall shiver with cold and fright. But things will happen to us so that we don't know ourselves. Cool, unlying life will rush in."

D. H. Lawrence

There is a peace that lies untouched in the California hills. It was a difficult place to leave.

Eventually, though, it was time, and we prepared to say goodbye to that small campground outside of San Francisco. The old couple from the neighboring RV came over to our bus to talk. The wife was direct and assertive and eager to tell me that when she first pulled up and saw we had four children, her heart sank. But she gushed over the kids, collecting their names and ages like butterflies to pin on a board, saying over and over again how well-behaved they were, how she couldn't believe the HOURS they played quietly at the picnic table between our two vehicles.

Her husband stood quietly behind her, tossing one-word interjections into the conversations (disarmed grenades). She mostly rolled her eyes at him or waved her hand, as if he was a pesky fly. They watched as I hooked up the van. They waved as we drove away, though we'd only spoken to them for about five minutes.

The mountains of California shed their houses as we drove up and east. Altitude: 2000 feet. The trees grew tall and straight, cedars or pines or some other evergreen. In the distance, we saw snow-covered peaks.

Sam, our youngest, only 2 1/2 years old, remained our scenery buff. When the bus was still, he terrorized us with his sticks and his loud, growling shouts of "Show yourself, Red Rackham!" But when the bus moved, and we wheezed up into the mountains, and Maile and I started shouting for the kids to come and look at the amazing sights, he was the first to come shooting up the bus aisle, launching on to the sofa or the booth, staring out the massive windows.

Long after the other kids lost interest, he sat there, arms resting on the narrow window sill, nose pressed up against the glass, constantly imploring me to take some dirt road or to get closer to the edge of the bridge. Every mountain was a 'cano (volcano). Every narrow river stream was a waterfall. In other words, he lived in a perpetual state of amazement, enraptured by the journey we so bravely took through a land of volcanoes and waterfalls.

We stopped close to the peak – Altitude 7200 feet. The shadowy ground off in the evergreens was covered in an icy layer of snow. I could only imagine how deep the snow must have been at one point, if small drifts of it survived to see that 70-degree day. Massive rocks bigger than our bus poked through the ground like broken bones. Whispers whisked through the trees, secrets I could only know by following them into the shadows.

I took in a deep breath of the cold air and walked back to the bus, leaving those secrets to be discovered on some other journey.

Then, we descended back to earth. We stopped at a truck stop to spend the night. I stepped out of the bus for a breath of fresh air. Some sort of beaming light at the back of the bus attracted my attention. I walked toward the west, toward the mountains we had just crossed over.

It was the sun, dropping down behind the Sierra Nevada mountain range. Great clouds of dust billowed around us.

Abra watching the world go by.

"Traveling is a brutality. It forces you to trust strangers and to lose sight of all that familiar comfort of home and friends. You are constantly off balance. Nothing is yours except the essential things – air, sleep, dreams, the sea, the sky – all things tending towards the eternal or what we imagine of it."

Cesare Pavese

Nevada contained inconceivable stretches of wilderness. Salt flats and brush and distant, crumbling mountains felt endless, like some kind of blue funk you can't quite shake. But there was also something serene about mile after empty mile – a peaceful longing that made me want to pull the bus over, buy 1,000 acres for $6,000 (as the signs offered), and build a small shack in which to spend the rest of my days.

There was something the opposite of serene when the bus's temperature gauge crept upward on every uphill stretch. There was an internal tension, a focus of will power. But still it moved up over 200. 205. 210.

Then, the red light blinked on. The bus shut off. Since it was impossible to coast to the side of the road while going uphill (at a snail's pace to begin with), I put on the parking brake, the four-ways, and turned off the engine. I parked in the right hand lane of a two-lane highway.

And there we sat. Sixty feet of vehicle. You might as well have dropped a mobile home on I-80.

I have many responses to things going wrong. Sometimes I run around like the proverbial chicken, bouncing from one possible remedy to the next. Sometimes I sulk, entering that endless wasteland. Sometimes I lay awake at night, my brain on overdrive. Worry is usually the fuel on which all of these responses feed.

But when the bus overheated, there was only one thing we could do: wait.

We waited as the tractor-trailers flew by, shaking us with their passage. We waited as tiny cars we had passed some time ago whirred along. We waited.

So often, I try to busy myself to avoid the waiting, and in that busyness, I miss so many of the things I could have learned, had I embraced the wait. I miss out on life by filling it up with artificial distractions.

After the diagnosis.

After the rejection.

After the failure.

Then, something beautiful: in the midst of the waiting, and the pain, and the disappointment, I find something. Maybe it's just a small yellow flower growing in the shade cast by a rock. Maybe it's another way forward. Maybe it's a different opportunity.

Or maybe it's an unopened container of coolant in the belly of the bus.

"It was like when you make a move in chess and just as you take your finger off the piece, you see the mistake you've made, and there's this panic because you don't know yet the scale of disaster you've left yourself open to."

Kazuo Ishiguro

There is that moment in time when you know everything is about to go horribly wrong. It's that feeling that comes just after the doctor tells you something unimaginable, or when your car starts sliding on the ice, or when someone looks at you and you realize they are choking. It's when you understand and believe that all the terrible things that happen in the world actually could happen. They do happen. And one of them is happening to you.

Thursday, May 17th. We drove down a 10% grade (think very, very steep). The bus would not stay in first gear – it kept kicking up to second, forcing me to use my brakes. Each time I pushed on the brakes, the air pressure dropped, and dropped, and dropped.

Suddenly, my foot was flat against the floor, and the brake would not stop us. I brought my other foot over. I pushed as hard as I could on the brake with two feet, pulled on the steering wheel to try and leverage my weight.

"Can you stop?" Maile asked me, a tremor in her voice.

We were only going ten miles per hour, but that was increasing, and soon we would be going much, much faster. I looked up at her quickly. I didn't say anything. I just shook my head, no, and tried to push the brake harder. Nothing. Ahead of us, the road curved to the left. Beyond the road, a thousand feet of air and rock and evergreens. Beyond that, the town, like a tiny model village. Far beyond that, more snow-capped mountains.

We drove through the Teton Pass, 8472 feet above sea level. And our brakes no longer worked.

Thirty minutes before that, we had climbed the Teton Pass, amazed by the view. The mountains' peaks, a harsh mixture of rock and ice, split the clouds. Warnings of a 10% grade didn't alarm me, although they would be almost double the highest grade (6%) we had encountered up to that point.

We had stopped two or three times on the way up to let the bus's engine cool. The angle of the road began to unsettle me – creeping along at 5 to 10 miles per hour up that mountain, sometimes it felt

188

like the bus could simply stop and coast backward. Eventually, we made it to the top.

The view was like nothing we had seen on our trip. The mountain peak, over 13,000 feet up (5,000 feet above us), was covered in evergreens, a hearty, rugged color broken only by the rock faces of cliffs. I wasn't looking forward to the trip down the mountain, but I determined to keep it in first gear and ignore anyone behind us who got upset about our tortoise-like pace. They would just have to deal with it.

"You have to jump into disaster with both feet."

Chuck Palahniuk

We had pulled away from the scenic view at the top of Teton Pass. Breathless. Anxious. Eager to have the ensuing four-mile descent behind us.

It wasn't long before I had realized we would be fortunate to make this stretch without incident. Even in first gear, I had to use my brakes too often, too hard. The air pressure dropped. The brakes smelled hot after just half a mile.

I pulled into a side pull-off area to give the bus a rest, and my parking brake barely engaged. Adrenaline left me feeling shaky. I opened the bus door. The cold air felt great, and behind us, the mountainside was covered in snow, but both were contrasted by the smell of hot brakes. The smell of something important not going well.

190

After ten minutes or so, I released the brake and began creeping forward. The brakes felt okay, but not quite right. I had no idea what to do, but then, I saw another pull-off a few hundred yards ahead. I decided to pull in there and park for an hour, let the brakes cool completely. We might take all day getting down. Oh, well.

By now, Maile and the three older kids sat just behind me. Sam napped in the back. The kids chattered on and on about the view, the trees, and the bears they wanted to see. It was surreal – inside, I felt a massive sense of tension nearing panic, yet just behind me the kids were having a great trip. They had no idea.

But Maile – I could tell she knew what was going on. She asked me short questions in a quiet voice as we crept along at 5 mph, questions that I had no answer for.

"Are we okay?"

"Can you stop?"

"Should we pull off?"

I pulled our 20,000 pounds into that next pull-off, preparing to stop, put on the parking brake, and wait until the brakes cooled. But it was at that moment I realized we couldn't stop, at least not completely. I pushed the brake all the way to the floor, but we kept coasting, a snail's pace really. It's amazing how immense fear can rise up in the face of such slow movement. In a last ditch effort, I pulled on the parking brake, but it did nothing. We kept coasting forward.

I had no other option but to coast back out on to the road. This is when we began gaining speed. This is when I reached over with my other foot, put both feet on the brake and pushed down as hard as I could. This is when I realized we could not stop.

A guardrail defined the next curve, to the left, just a hundred yards or so ahead of us. Beyond that road, a thousand feet of air and rock and evergreens.

Faster. Soon, we were going fifteen miles per hour. We came around the turn. I began calculating at what point I would need to wreck the bus into the side of the mountain. The brakes no longer slowed us at all. Then, we saw it – on the left, a runaway truck ramp, the kind I used to always look at and think, Seriously? People actually use those?

"Should we go in there?" Maile asked me. I didn't want to. For a second, my mind weighed up the costs – getting stuck on the ramp, having to get a tow truck. Surely things hadn't gotten that bad? Then, in that same second, my brain calculated the alternative: there was no alternative. We couldn't stop.

A few cars flew past us on their way up the mountain. A large gap in the sparse traffic let me cross to the left hand lane. We approached the runaway truck ramp. I committed to it, veering to the left. We hit the ramp at 15-20 mph, and the bus quickly sank into the loose gravel.

We ground to a stop among the stones of the runaway truck ramp. My hands shook as I took them away from the steering wheel and placed them in my lap. My legs trembled as they let off the pedal, and the burning smell of brakes caught up to us, enveloped us from behind, reminded us of how bad it might have been.

I looked back at Maile. Her eyes seemed stuck open, unblinking.

"That could have been really, really, really bad," she said, her voice wavering.

I swallowed. Nodded.

She took the kids to the back of the bus and turned on a movie. I went out and walked around the bus. Smoke came out from behind the front wheels. So relatively slow had our approach to the runaway truck ramp been, and so effective the 8-inch thick layer of loose pebbles in slowing us, that the bus hadn't even gone all the way in. Our back tires were still on pavement.

I looked out over the incredible view again – the trees and the cliffs and the mountains. Everything was completely still. Peaceful. I inhaled the air, and it was like drinking icy cold water.

The next few hours passed in a post-adrenaline haze. The nicest officer in the world stopped and made sure we were okay, then called for the largest wrecker they could find. He invited me to sit in his car while he wrote up the report. Every once in a while, he looked at me without saying a word, then shook his head in amazement and looked away. After doing that two or three times, he finally spoke.

"You do realize how lucky you are, right? How bad that could have been?"

I nodded, feeling a bit choked up, and looked out the window, up the mountain, in the direction from which we had come.

A few hours later, the truck arrived. Two men were in it. One of them, a long-haired mountain man with a six-inch goatee and a few missing teeth, stared up into the bus at Maile.

"Everyone okay?" he asked in a genuine voice.

She nodded.

"White-knuckled it there for a bit, I guess?" He spoke a language I understood: kindness.

She nodded again, biting her lip.

We waited in the minivan at the bottom of the mountain and took a picture of the truck as it brought Willie down to us. After a long

194

discussion with the tow-truck driver, and testing the brakes, we went on our merry way. By then it was past 5pm, but we thought we'd still try to make it to Yellowstone, a few hours away.

Just outside of Jackson Hole, a herd of bison crossed the road in front of us. The kids all crowded to the front. The huge beasts, from some other time period, lumbered slowly up on to the asphalt, then into the huge expanse of grass on the other side. It was beautiful. Breathtaking. Surreal.

Out of this silence spoke Cade, our prophet, and he summed up the whole day in one sentence.

"We must be the luckiest family in the world."

The runaway truck ramp that probably saved our lives.

Here you can see Willie hitching a ride to the bottom of the
Teton Pass. Part of the Teton mountain range is in the
background. Three months later a trucker would lose his
brakes coming down the pass, crash at this very corner, and
lose his life.

Buffalo cross the highway in front of us somewhere north of Jackson and less than an hour after our Teton Pass experience.

"Most things I worry about never happen anyway."
Tom Petty

But Maile didn't find herself thinking that we were the luckiest family in the world. Here's her take on the wild ride down the Teton Pass, and where she ended up (metaphorically speaking).

Maile

I sat in the booth, facing forward, looking over Shawn's shoulder and out the panoramic windows at the front of the bus. While Sammy napped in the bed in the back room, the three older kids sat beside and opposite me, noses pressed to the glass of the side windows. They "ohhhed" and "awwwed" over the green and white landscape rising and falling around us like some interactive cyclorama.

Beauty can overwhelm you sometimes; it bowled us over that day. The road to these mountains had winded through valleys and brief prairies that reached out and grabbed the breath right out of my lungs.

"This is too beautiful," I kept saying, hand over my mouth, trying to keep a little air for myself.

Then, we began the climb up Teton Pass. While we gasped and pointed at the arrowhead shaped evergreens standing like a majestic army at attention and spanning the snowy peaks of the mountain, Willie wheezed and puttered up the 10% grade road leading always up and always higher. We marveled, not giving thought to the path down this mountain.

We've managed to do that this entire trip: not look too far ahead.

When the road crested and began its steep and windy descent, Shawn pulled Willie back to the lowest gear, easing the bus's heavy frame slowly downward. But soon Willie whined and lurched forward to the next gear, gaining speed one quick mph after another. So Shawn would press the brakes pulling the reins in, the brake light on the dashboard blazing orange.

My eyes forgot the scenery, the soldiers saluting us outside. Instead, my eyes rested on the orange light flashing on and off from below the steering wheel. I don't know much about vehicular mechanics, but I know that you can't ride your brakes on a mountain. Shawn knew that, too. At the next gravelly pull-off, he eased Willie over and put on the parking brake. "We'll just wait here till the brakes cool off a little," he announced from the front seat.

"Yeah, good idea," I replied. We'd just take it slow and easy down the mountain; we were in no hurry.

So we waited. The kids chattered about the snow, wishing for boots and gloves, eager to frolic in the last remnants of winter. I sat there, eager for the valley at the bottom of the mountain, for flat roads, for the sight of a small Wyoming town blooming with bustle in the spring.

With a high whistle from Willie, Shawn released the parking brake, inched back onto the road. But soon Willie began complaining and jolted into the next gear; again the orange light flashed on the dashboard. We saw another pull off coming up on the right. Shawn steered Willie toward it, his foot pressing further down on the brake pedal, but we felt its effect less and less. Shawn pulled the parking brake once we reached the gravelly patch.

Nothing. The parking brake didn't work.

I saw Shawn's second foot join the brake pedal, his full body weight pressed upon that rectangular piece of metal. But still we moved forward, gaining speed slowly and steadily.

"Can you stop?" I asked, trying to disguise the panic in my voice from the children. He shook his head, bracing himself between the black cushion of the driver's seat and the brake pedal solid against the floor.

And that's when the shaking began, inside of me and outside of me. My hands began to tremor, my legs jittered as I stood up from the booth and walked toward the front of the bus.

"Hey, guys, why don't you take a seat, okay?" I said nonchalantly to the kids, eyes never leaving Shawn's two feet. Eager questions unraveled from their mouths, but I paid no attention.

It's funny but my first thought was, "How can I get the kids off this bus?" Sometimes, I wonder if I'm a good enough mom, if I really love them like I should. And then a moment like that comes and they are my first concern; I know I must protect them.

But getting off the bus was out of the question. We were moving too quickly to open the door and jump out. While my eyes scanned the road before us, my mind was already a mile ahead, imagining the worst. But while my mind ushered our souls through the pearly gates of heaven, my eyes spied the emergency runaway ramp that appeared to our left.

"Babe, what about the runaway ramp?" I suggested as calmly as possible.

"I'm gonna have to use it," Shawn replied, still straining against the brake.

Traffic came towards us on the left, so we had to wait for a clearing, hope for a clearing, before veering over.

Then, it came. In seconds, Willie's unhindered wheels came to an abrupt stop in the deep stones on the runaway ramp.

And there we sat, the engine running, the bus still, and the kids smiling. I sat down at the booth, the wobbly foundation of my legs unable to hold me up any longer.

I don't even remember the words we spoke after that. And I don't remember relief or thankfulness rushing over me. No, I just felt scared. Really, really scared.

Later on, we drove down the rest of the mountain in our minivan while a tow truck pulled Willie to safety in the valley below the Teton Pass. As we coasted around the remaining 2 miles of curves and steep grade that the mountain offered, we realized how close disaster had been. If Willie had given out just 40 yards later than he did, we would have crashed, either into or over the side of the mountain. There were no manageable pull-offs or runaway ramps to help us for the rest of the way down.

That was a sobering thought.

Funny enough, you would think this experience would bolster my faith. But it actually left me questioning a lot. The next day, I wrote this to God in my journal:

"I try to explain away instances like yesterday. Immediately, I excuse it to 'chance' because there are a lot of people in this world who don't have an

emergency ramp show up just in the nick of time. So Your love is either fickle, or had nothing to do with yesterday, or doesn't exist. Because here's the hard part: I don't know if I could have found Your love in the scenario that would have presented itself if that ramp hadn't been there. That thirty seconds was lonely, God. It was scary."

So here I now sit in this tension: awed by the beauty of this world yet terrified by its ugliness, ceaselessly thankful that we made it safely down the mountain yet baffled by a God that sometimes doesn't provide the emergency ramp.

I want to understand that God.

This is Sam contemplating life and the Grand Teton
Mountain range after our brush with death.

> **"Nights are long when it's cold and you're waiting for a train."**
>
> **J.M.G. Le Clezio**

We pulled into Yellowstone at 8:45 pm, and the fading adrenaline rush from losing our brakes only six hours before left me feeling exhausted. The south entrance to Yellowstone National Park had only opened a week before, and the roads were lined with piles of snow pushed aside for the new season.

Elk and buffalo wandered through the most beautiful valleys I had ever seen, but it was getting dark, and registration closed at 9 pm, so we drove straight to the campground, picked up our information, and slowly directed the bus to where we would (thankfully) remain parked for about a week.

It was dark. Maile helped me back in to the fifty-foot long space. I shut down the bus and smiled with relief at Maile as she came back on board, cold air swirling in behind her.

"We made it," I said.

She nodded. She looked exhausted. I couldn't wait to hook the bus up to electric, turn on the heat, perhaps take a hot shower, eat some hot food, and then go to sleep. My hands still shook when I thought about how close we had come to disaster. It made me sick to my stomach.

I grabbed a small flashlight and walked outside. It was cold! I tried to make a lot of noise in order to scare off any Grizzlies hiding in the shadows. I unwound the massive electrical cord and plugged it into the outlet in the post, then went back into the bus.

Nothing. No electricity. I checked the breaker box, made sure we weren't overloading the circuits, and went back out. I flipped the switch on and off. I tried a different outlet. I double-checked the breakers again.

But no matter what I did, we weren't getting any electricity. I tried to turn the bus back on – we couldn't run it all night, but we could perhaps keep it on just long enough to take hot showers. But the bus battery was dead. The engine wouldn't turn over.

Maile looked like she was going to weep. I helped the kids into the warmest pajamas they had and made beds on the floor of our bedroom (it was pitch black, and they were too scared to sleep in their bunks). Maile and I changed clothes with the help of the flashlight. We didn't say much to each other that night – only a few sentences.

"What are we going to do if we can't get the electric to work?" Maile whispered at one point.

I thought for a moment.

"We'll have to go home," I whispered. "We can't live on this thing without electricity, and we can't afford to stay at hotels every night."

Silence. Eventually, all six of us slept.

When I woke up, my nose was freezing cold. The kids were still sleeping, buried under their blankets. But Maile wasn't in bed beside me. I looked toward the front of the bus, and there she was, sitting in the passenger seat, her feet propped up on the dash. In the next instant, she came walking back to the room.

"Let's go, everyone wake up."

I groaned.

"But it's freezing out there."

"We've got to get this figured out or start driving home," she said. "I can't take this anymore."

So I pried myself out from under the covers. I could tell she was ticked off. But something had entered my brain just before I fell asleep the previous night.

"I just remembered that there's an electrical box behind the refrigerator. Maybe we flipped one of the breakers in that box."

So we tried to pull the fridge out of its spot, but it was wedged in place and difficult to move. Finally, I used the backside of a hammer to grip the bottom of the fridge, and we gave it an almighty yank, and it came sliding out. I shined my flashlight on the breakers. One was flipped.

Five minutes later, Mai was in the shower, heat billowed through the vents, and oatmeal was in the microwave. Catastrophe averted. Next order of business? Explore Yellowstone.

Sam, Lucy, Abra and Cade (still in pajamas) acting goofy
along the Yellowstone Grand Canyon.

"I'll just tell you what I remember because memory is as close as I've gotten to building my own time machine."

Samantha Hunt

The woman who still feels like a girl sometimes tires of digging through the bottom of the bus for the kids' shoes or wondering if the next Laundromat will have a change machine. The man who still feels like a boy is weary of emptying the waste tank and worrying about getting the bus stuck. The third month of a four-month trip is the 21st mile of a marathon.

The woman looks for a movie for the kids while the man makes popcorn. She bends over and sweeps Legos out of the way, then opens the small drawer under the couch. The man pinches her butt. She laughs and looks over her shoulder.

"What movie are you picking, Mom?" one of the four kids shouts.

They have been in very close quarters for over ninety days. Moments of intimacy for the parents are few and far between. The man gives the woman a signal.

Meet me in the back in two minutes.

They walk back the long bus hall, closing the two doors. They are giddy, like high schoolers trying to find a place to park late at night. Unfortunately, the bedroom door has a gaping hole in the bottom where a large vent used to be, so the man blocks it with an oversized plastic storage container. It seemed like a good idea at the time.

She moves the dirty clothes on to the floor, and he jumps into bed. More Legos greet him, like tiny sea urchins. They sigh and pull back the sheets and pick out the Legos and doll clothes and Matchbox cars.

When the bed is clear, they lay down. He smiles. She smiles. He kisses her. Then, they hear the tiniest of voices from the other side of the storage bin blocking the door. He looks over his shoulder, and a small head peaks up through the narrow space.

"Guysh, what are you doing?" It is their four-year old. She has long blond hair and blue eyes, and her s's come out like sh's (think Sid from *Ice Age*). She wants a drink. The man shakes his head in disbelief.

"How do you even fit through there?" he asks, walking toward the door.

"Are you guysh naked in there?" she asks them.

He tries not to laugh. She keeps asking questions.

"Did you lock the door sho that no one would shee you when you're naked?" she asks again.

"I wish," he says, leaning down and pushing her head gently back through the vent. "Now, go ask your brother for a drink. And don't come back in here until the door is open. Understand?"

"Of coursh."

He goes back to the bed and lies down beside the woman. And suddenly the woman and man are boy and girl again. They look at each other – she giggles, and he laughs. They hold hands and stare at the ceiling. She suddenly remembers, in the time it takes a lightning bug to flash on and off, that this is the greatest adventure of their life together. He recalls the first time they held hands in that move theatre in Camp Hill, PA. He remembers how he hadn't wanted to be anywhere but there.

They hear the voices of their children in the front of the bus: how'd it happen so fast? How could those two people holding hands fifteen years before be in any way connected to these very different but same people, holding hands in Yellowstone while their four children argue over popcorn rights in the front of the bus?

Outside, a few miles away, herds of bison and elk wander through Haydn Valley. A bear swims through icy Yellowstone River, her cub following desperately behind. Downstream, water crashes through the gorge, wearing away another layer of time.

But in the big blue bus, for just a moment, time has stopped.

"He has no talent at all, that boy! You, who are his friend, tell him, please, to give up painting."

--Manet to Monet, regarding Renoir

You will want to give up.

When you're not even that far from home and you're already stuck in a ditch. When your sense of adventure slams up against the inevitable reality of bills and homesickness and costs you couldn't have budgeted for.

You will want to give up. Don't.

When your best work falls short and the words don't flow, you'll think of your bed back at home. You'll remember the comfort of predictability, the safety of not trying, the ease of a life in which nothing is at stake.

You will want to give up. Don't.

When you realize that nothing is working out as you expected. When you start to wonder if adventure is just another word for irresponsibility. When you doubt everything that at one time seemed so clear – when you start to feel the need to conform to the expectations of everyone around you.

You will want to give up. Don't

When your popcorn maker burns out. When you run out of Sour Skittles. When you get lost and one part of your adventure takes twice as long as it should. When you get sick and tired of emptying everyone else's waste.

You will want to give up. Don't.

When your brakes give out and you're losing control. When your electricity doesn't work and you fall asleep in a cold, silent, simmering anger. When you drive all day and don't find what you're looking for.

You will want to give up. Don't.

When previous failures push fear to the surface. When each and every hill makes you wonder if there's a runaway truck ramp. When the kids won't stop talking, or you and your spouse can't stop fighting, or you start to wish there HADN'T been a runaway truck ramp.

You will want to give up. Don't.

216

Because if you had given up before, you wouldn't be where you are. You wouldn't have what you have. You wouldn't be who you have become. So don't give up now. Your future self will thank you for persevering.

The greatest adventure is what lies ahead.
Today and tomorrow are yet to be said.
The chances, the changes are all yours to make.
The mold of your life is in your hands to break.

J.R.R. Tolkien

Maile

As Shawn and I drove into the serene foliage of the campground where Willie
would rest for the next 5 days, my nerves draped over every millimeter of my
body like live wires, jumping and sparking with the slightest brush of contact.
Willie had just accomplished the daring feat of driving down yet another steep
grade during our descent into this village at the base of Mt. Rushmore.

In the weeks since our incident on the Teton Pass, every slight undulation on
each road we traveled caused me to breathe in short, machine gun bursts and
sweat profusely. So this path to Mt. Rushmore, littered with sizable hills and
curves that forced Shawn to rely on Willie's unreliable brakes, kept me in a
complete state of panic.

Thankfully, coming into town, we had no incidents. We learned after Teton that Willie brakes a lot better without the added weight of towing our minivan behind him. Hence, on every 6% grade hill or higher, we got into the practice of taking the van off. I drove the van down the hill with the kids while Shawn drove Willie.

But honestly, I was tired of the worry. Every time I kissed Shawn through the open driver's side window of the minivan and watched him walk away toward Willie, I thought it would be our last. Of course, my imagination provided the Richard Marx ballad for background music and reeled back the action of Shawn's walk so everything was in slow mo and saturated with emotion. So I'd drive down the hill, crying into my shoulder (as to not alarm the children) while whispering unintelligible pleas to God, if He was even up there or even cared.

Of course, every time we made it safely to the bottom.

So by the time we got to Mt. Rushmore, I felt I couldn't take one more mountain or hill or 7% grade. And unfortunately, we had a little bit of all of that to face when we would leave this town in 5 days time.

All week, the worry lingered about a quarter inch above my head, a moving cartoon cloud complete with rain and lightning. I kept busy with the kids and cooking and monument-viewing, but the cloud hovered. My mom flew into Rapid City to stay with us on the bus for a few days. As I drove to the airport to pick her up (the very roads we'd be driving in a few days' time), I memorized every incline and decline, every turn and stoplight, judging each based on their potential trouble for Willie's brakes.

219

The evening of our departure arrived. My stomach felt corseted while the armpits of my t-shirt turned dark with perspiration. My kids, my mom, and I loaded up in the minivan, and Shawn came over for his farewell kiss.

As we drove away, my mom listened as I gave her a rundown of the potential hazards ahead of us. About two miles into the drive, she managed to steer the conversation to other topics, occasionally shouting to the back of the van to get the kids opinions on this or that. She seemed completely unconcerned.

That, my friends, is the blessing of distraction. Because while I still felt frightened and worried, seeing my mom calm and cheerful gave me hope that perhaps everything might just be okay. She kept me from evaporating into a steam cloud of "what if's"; she kept me present in the safe, forward motion of a minivan driving down a highway with the excited chatter of 4 children and their adoring Meme.

And you know what? We made it down the mountain.

> "And that's the wonderful thing about family travel: it provides you with experiences that will remain locked forever in the scar tissue of your mind."

Dave Barry

It was Monday night, and we parked the bus at a truck stop somewhere outside Des Moines. I sat in the passenger seat feeling tired and irritable, playing some game or other on my iPhone. The sun, gone from the sky, left a wake of color where it had just been shining bright and hot a few minutes ago.

I suppose there were many tangible reasons for my irritability that night: a desire to be home (wherever that was), anxiety about the future, and three and a half months in cramped quarters with five other people (all of whom have many more reasons to be irritated with me than I do with them). Worrying about wastewater tanks and fresh water tanks and the money required to keep Willie running.

But emerging in my mind was an unsettled feeling, something new. Something that had been gaining ground as the trip progressed. Something beyond my own circumstances.

It had started to make itself known in a tangible way a few days ago when we were in Sioux Falls, SD, and we approached the on-ramp of the highway. A forlorn man had stood there on the corner. He looked rather pitiful, like a homeless person who had tried to dress up and fallen horribly short. His hair looked combed, but in a way that made me think it wasn't combed often. He looked self-conscious about his current state. As we drove up, I noticed he held a cardboard sign. I expected the sign to say something like, "Homeless, need money." But the words I saw scratched in black marker put a lump in my throat.

"Worthington" was written across the top, and "Daughter's Graduation" was written along the bottom.

Worthington is a town in Minnesota, about 60 miles away from where we were parked. And that night, as I sat there playing some meaningless game on my iPhone, I wished I would have taken the afternoon and driven him there. Two hours out of my life. I wondered if someone going to Worthington (or that general direction) had taken him. Or if perhaps, at some graduation ceremony, a girl had scanned the crowd, disappointed because once again her father had not come.

Then, later that night, as we drove to a Ruby Tuesday's to use a gift card some friends had given us, we passed another person, a woman this time, standing at another intersection.

"Stranded. Need food," the black magic marker had written on her strip of cardboard. And again my heart caught in my throat. And my jaw clenched. And I drove on by. We went to Ruby's and had a good meal, and my youngest cried about his dessert, and I found myself disappointed with what I had ordered.

But my stomach was full, and I wouldn't have to worry about food until the next morning when I would look through the fridge and eat whatever I wanted to eat.

Why didn't I stop the van and take her along?

Again and again, poverty called out to me on this trip. More than at any other time in my life. Maybe it's because I was out of my routine and my eyes were open. I looked around. I was more aware. I was in surroundings that I did not take for granted.

Again and again, I was sorely disappointed by my response, which basically was confusion, or uncertainty, or a willingness that came far too late. My automatic reaction to those in need was skepticism or distrust. Which was especially sad, considering that I have spent the last 35 years in church. 35 years going at least once a week, and up to four times a week, to a place where people meet who have dedicated their lives to following Christ. Yet after all of those years, I still didn't know how to respond to poverty.

Of course, I didn't blame the church. I blamed me. I'd like to say that day was the last time. Never again would I encounter poverty without doing something. Anything.

Yet, that felt like so many empty promises, and I was left there, in the passenger seat of a big blue bus, and the sky was almost dark, and even after all of that, I didn't feel that I understood poverty any better.

"I'm playing with fire, with something I don't understand."

L.J. Smith

We all know when we're in the middle of a fire.

I'm not talking about the wood-burning kind made up of super-hot flames. I'm talking about the kind of fire that rages on the inside, an emotional fire, the kind that leads some people to anger and others to depression. The kind of fire that leaves you second-guessing your purpose or your current direction. Or maybe it's a fire that feels like it's destroying your life through loss or disappointment or failure.

Sometimes, it smolders. Sometimes, it blazes through in a flash.

I can always tell when I'm in the middle of one of these fires because I start to do things that are completely unlike me. Things like getting angry at a Best Western customer service person because they told me the wrong price. Things like wanting to ram my Mac down the Mac store person's throat because the only reason I bought AppleCare was because the woman who sold me the computer implied that it covered accidental damage. It doesn't cover accidental damage, and now, I'm looking at $700 worth of repairs and weighing up whether or not throwing the Mac up against their shiny glass storefront would feel good enough to compensate for the additional financial hit I would take due to, you know, vandalism and stuff.

These are theoretical examples, of course.

The fire rages in our lives, and in its wake, we are left feeling disappointed, bitter, angry, or depressed. Or all four. Or something else. The landscape of our life begins to feel charred and dead. Worthless. Mordor-like.

At Yellowstone National Park, I made my first acquaintance with Lodgepole Pines. A hardy species, they grow in high elevations and close together. So close together, in fact, that they thin each other out, and the dead trees fall over, leaning against the live ones. This may seem insignificant, but when a fire comes through, the leaning, dead trees provide a kind of kindling that allows the fire to race to the top of the tree line, obliterating every single tree from top to bottom.

The bark is also thin, lessening its resistance to heat and flames. You could say that these trees are, in some ways, built to facilitate their own death by fire.

But there's one other thing about the Lodgepole Pine, something important, and it has to do with its pine cone. This particular cone is a prickly little son-of-a-gun, and a sticky, sappy adhesive holds it tightly shut, enclosing its seeds. The cones fall and gather on the forest floor, up to 50,000 per acre each year, but no new trees can grow because the cones are glued shut. Nothing can open them.

Well, one thing can.

Fire.

And when that fire comes, it blazes through the Lodgepole Pines. It races up the deadwood, devouring every single tree, leaving nothing but charred, black stumps behind. Nothing but ash and death.

But it also opens up all of those pine cones, leaving millions of released seeds behind, and the seeds fall into the rich soil, and the rain and the sunlight, which can now come through, lift up a new generation of life.

This is what that internal fire will do for me, if I let it. It will (painfully) remove all the existing brush and deadwood and even, horror upon horrors, the living things. The things I've spent so much time growing and nurturing. But it also releases all the seeds of life that were stuck inside of me, the ideas and the emotions and the plans that never would have come to fruition without the fire. Without the destruction.

And the life that springs up out of that regeneration: that is the abundant life.

"The beginning is always today."

— Mary Shelley

"Well, here we are," I said as we pulled the big blue bus into yet another Walmart parking lot, this one just outside of Urbana, IL. "Home sweet home."

Maile smiled.

"I'm going to miss spending the night in Walmart parking lots," she said.

As silly as that sounded, I knew exactly what she meant. There was something nice about pulling into a mostly vacant parking lot, finding an out-of-the-way spot for the bus, turning on the generator, and falling asleep to the sound of its humming while a cool breeze whistles in through the screened window at the back of the bus. There was something nice about the knowledge that the next day we would be on the road again, to a new destination a few hundred miles away, and that, once again, we would see things and places and people we had never seen before.

A kind of reflective peace descended during the last few weeks of our trip. It was as if our emotions had decided to mirror the landscape, going from mountainous, rugged and ever-changing to smooth and even. It felt kind of like one long sigh.

Once home was in our sights, I found myself thinking back over the trip, marveling at the experience, hesitantly lifting rocks of thought and waiting to see what had grown there during the last three and a half months, waiting to see what might scurry out. Perhaps a new take on my current life. A new direction. New hope.

But even more often, I found myself looking forward. What waited for us when we returned to Lancaster? What sort of work would I be able to find? Did my novel have a future? Would we write a book about our trip? Would I be able to survive the summer eating only sweet corn?

So many questions. I was still working through a lot of things in my mind. Somehow, though, the adventure had (nearly) cured me of my need for answers. My need to know where the next project would come from or how I'd make any money. My need to know if God would supply another runaway truck ramp just in time.

For perhaps the first time in my life, I was okay living in the here and now. Let me tell you: it was a glorious feeling.

"When many voices are speaking at once, listen to the one most quiet and gentle. That's the one worth listening to."

Miranda Linda Weisz

Maile

Immediately after Shawn and I nearly met an untimely end coming down the mountain, I invited some distant acquaintances over to keep me company in the gray room of my mind. I tidied up, straightened the leather sofa and chair, stoked the fire to keep the room warm, too warm, uncomfortably warm. I knew that's how these folks liked it.

And they arrived, a noisy bunch, in wrinkled clothes of muted tones, hair unwashed and tangled. And their greetings as they walked through the door were different yet always the same:

"He can't be trusted."
"He isn't good."

"He won't show up when you need Him most."

"He doesn't care about you or anyone else."

"He's selfish."

They filed in with this wrangle of words filling every corner, every crevice of my sweltering room. Every corner but one.

For in that corner sat a mysterious woman with large eyes and a knowing smile. She nodded politely to all of my guests, who in turn ignored her and urged their voices louder. I ignored her as well. I didn't know how she got there and simply didn't care why she stayed; my only focus was the deep satisfaction I was receiving from this cacophony around me, the hopeless drowning sensation it gave to my soul, the satisfying scratching that feels like relief while tearing flesh and summoning blood.

Without the slightest encouragement from me, she swept up next to me as I bent over the fire, throwing dead log after dead log onto an already billowing fire. And in the heat of the flame, she whispered in my ear, "But is it really true?"

I wasn't surprised by her question. I'd been waiting the whole time for her to rise and ask it. But I recoiled in disgust, spitting back at her, "As a matter of fact, it is!" Rushing away, I looked for an open chair, a place to escape her inappropriate questions. The only available seat was the one she just left; I nearly ran toward it and huddled in its corner.

Always persistent, she followed me while the clamor of my guests continued, a constant tone-deaf chorus that was ever so slightly getting on my nerves. I sensed

232

her kneeling beside me though I kept my eyes averted, staring at the shimmering silver paint on the walls.

This time, I didn't wait for a question; I asked one of my own: "And what would have happened had the emergency ramp not been there? Tell me that."

Without so much as a breath between my statement and hers, she replied, "But it was, Maile; it was."

Smoldering, I sat silent. She was another one of those "positive thinkers," those "glass is always half-full" types, and I didn't like it. But then she spoke again.

"Tell me this: Has the emergency ramp ever not been there? Has the 'bad thing' ever happened?"

These questions startled me. For the first time in our conversation, I looked directly at her. Tears softly gathered in the corners of her large eyes, swelling then breaking in gentle ribbons down the smooth terrain of her cheeks. She already knew the answer.

"Yes," I whispered, my voice stumbling and uneven. "My dad leaving, my parents' divorce, my miscarriage, our failed business, the loss of our home…" There were so many disappointments and losses. So much pain. The list kept growing, and yet with each situation, I presented, she knew it, not just the name, but the details. She knew the devastation, the indescribable ache, the unquenchable hunger.

Suddenly, I realized the quietness of the room. A sensible fire crackled on the hearth, and my raucous guests had left. As I surveyed the empty yet cozy room, I heard her whisper once more in my ear: "Is it true?"

No, it wasn't true. He was not deceitful or unkind or evil or selfish. No, in each and every one of those situations, He had proven Himself to be good and loving and worthy of my trust:

He gave me the evidence of miracles in the now-restored marriage of my parents.

He filled my empty and aching arms with a beautiful, blue-eyed girl named Abra.

He ushered our family into our most exciting era yet as my husband began pursuing his dream to be a writer.

And in the absence of a house, He gave me a whole country to explore and taste and enjoy.

When I looked up from my pondering, I found myself alone, tranquil and content, while staring into a mirror with those kind and wondering eyes gazing back at me.

"Travel is more than the seeing of sights; it is a change that goes on, deep and permanent, in the ideas of living."

Miriam Beard

I am not very good at waiting.

When I was a kid, I ran everywhere. I ran out to get the mail and ran to answer the door and tried to run while pushing the lawn mower around the yard so I could finish and move on to the next thing. I ran to our neighbors if I had time to play, and I tried to run down the halls in middle school. If mom or dad asked me to get something outside, I ran.

I so badly wanted to be THERE. Not HERE.

You know where I mean. That place out there. That place where I'm making more money than I am now. That place where I have a little bit of a nicer house than I do now. That place where I'm finally married or I finally have more kids or the kids have finally

235

moved out. That place where all of my current problems are sorted out.

We're prodded into this mindset by the atmosphere of our age. Every retailer can help you figure out a way to get what you want NOW instead of waiting until you can afford it. We can view Super Bowl commercials before they even air on television, and we read spoilers of our favorite shows before they take place. We buy things now and pay for them later. Young kids want to be teenagers, teenagers want to be adults, and adults want to be retired.

I wrote about how this trip helped me live more in the here and now. And it did. But all it took was one bit of bad news, one unexpected disappointment, and suddenly, the here and now wasn't good enough anymore. HERE wasn't good enough. I wanted to be THERE.

The word "wait" shows up in the New Living Translation of the Bible 79 times. That's a lot of waiting. In one of those instances, Moses tells his people, "Stay here and wait for us until we come back to you." But the Israelites simply couldn't wait for Moses to return; they started feeling abandoned, so they created a god all their own. A lump of gold. And they worshiped it, and they bowed down to it, and they couldn't get enough of it.

I read that story, and I thought to myself, *How completely ridiculous — those Israelites sure had issues!* And then, I got to the place where I was tired of waiting and felt abandoned, and I created my own little gods. When God didn't show up in my timing, I rushed to put my hope in people or business plans or my own ingenuity, and soon, I clutched on to that thing like a golden calf, and I caressed it and maybe even called it "My precious."

That's a little weird.

"Be still in the presence of the LORD, and wait patiently for him to act." Psalm 37:7

Where should I wait? In his presence. To me, that's a meditative place, a deliberate place, a place where I can hear my own breathing. And what should I do in that space?

Be still.

Wait patiently.

Stop running.

"Travel is like death in that it requires separation and, indeed, mourning. And travel by sea, unlike the far more rapid air travel, gives time for mourning, separation, and loss as one sees space slowly open between ship and shore and watches the coastline recede and eventually disappear."

Philip H. Pfatteicher

I remember climbing up on to the roof of Grandma's house back in the mid-80s. I was eight or nine years old (the age of my oldest son now), and my teenage cousins reached down over the edge of the sandpaper-like asphalt shingles and pulled me up, scraping the skin off my stomach. I remember the giddy feeling of being so high, of looking down on the cornstalks that usually looked down on me.

There was something raw and wild about being on a roof, and as the sun set, we lay there on the shallow slope, our hands behind our heads, our feet braced to keep us from sliding off. Then, when all was dark, the fireworks launched into the night sky, their explosions thudding against my small rib cage like a defibrillator.

I was too young to wonder how my Grandma was feeling during those years after my Grandfather had died. Almost thirty years ago. I wonder if she cried herself to sleep, missing him or lay awake at night worrying about how she would pay the mortgage. I wonder if she heard those fireworks exploding and wished he was back for one last Fourth of July, sitting out on their small deck, smelling the cut hay and watching the fireflies.

My Grandma, my father's mother, always loved us with a tough and indefatigable love. Her kisses were direct and non-negotiable, always followed by a few firm slaps on the cheek or a vice-grip pinch on that fatty area under your chin. She had been sort of bony for most of the years that I remember her, but not frail. Anything but frail.

Ironic, then, that this tough love was always accompanied by a soft voice, kind eyes, and a clearly communicated message: your presence meant the world to her. Her love, after one of those signature greetings, came in the form of iced tea or a hot dinner. When I walked into her house (or, in recent years, her room), her reaction was always the same.

"Well!" she said, as if you presented her, not with just your presence, but with a check for $1 million. "Shawn, Shawn, Shawn. Look who it is. How are you? How are you?" Her voice came out in a sing-song kind of cadence, perhaps from all of those years of singing in church or with her children.

A text I got from my parents that night was a wake up call. When they walked into her room, there was no overwhelming welcome. She sat, and when she spoke it was with a quiet, weak voice. But she was 92, and her body had endured much, and her mind struggled to make all of the connections.

When I heard that, I knew it was time to head home.

To be sure, she has pushed on through overwhelming odds before: heart surgery, multiple strokes, a recent bout of pneumonia. But she seemed to be fading, and I wanted to be home with her and with my family. So we cut our trip short by a week or so and planned to head home from Indiana that Friday night: a 12-hour drive, and we would get home by Saturday night.

111 days down. Three to go. I hoped we would make it in time.

"It was awkward, revisiting a world you have never seen before: like coming home, after a long journey, to someone else's house."

Umberto Eco

Maile

So tonight, we begin the final leg of our journey. Two nights ago, Shawn and I sat across from each other (he on the couch, me in the booth) and decided that his grandma's failing health was the call beckoning us back a week earlier than we had intended.

It seems like such a small alteration to the plans: one week. But as I took a walk at our campground in rural Indiana after our decision, I felt so strange. By the end of the existing week, our trip would be over. My heart was fragmented with feeling:

Excitement (anticipating the tight hugs and grinning faces of so many folks that we love and miss.)

Regret (were there things left undone on this trip, moments I missed or didn't hold quite long enough?)

Sadness (when anything great ends, sadness is always an appropriate response.)

Celebration (when anything great ends, celebration is always an appropriate response.)

Fear (that our great adventure has come to an end; that a humdrum existence is all we can expect from here on out.)

I shared that last feeling with a friend over email yesterday. But as I wrote it, my fear dissipated; fear has gotten more feeble on this journey. So I wrote this to my friend: "But I also know that God is far more wild than that."

In the past 4 months, I've seen more beauty than in my entire life up to this point. It was holy yet tangled, majestic yet terrifying, serene yet treacherous. And I found myself often asking this question: "What kind of a God makes a creation like this?"

A wild one.

Two and a half years ago, our goal was to own a bigger house and a nicer car. But God was too good to leave us there. He dreamed bigger than us. So He gently as possible, laid us at rock bottom, stripping us of our biggest earthly possessions (my husband's business as well as our home) and calling us to the basement of my in-laws.

I remember the night after we discovered rock bottom. I awoke, my heart aching with questions and sadness. I lay on the floor beside our bed, my forehead buried in the carpet, my fists pressed against eyes, asking many questions of God. And as clearly as I've ever known anything, God told me this:

"What I'm doing is a gift."

Immediately, my response was "Well, it's a pretty shitty gift." I quickly learned how very wrong I was.

Today, we're still unwrapping that gift. It didn't show up the next morning on the kitchen table as a simple box wrapped in patterned paper with a stick-on bow. No, it's arrived in pieces over these years: multi-faceted and deliberate, strange and fantastic. Parts of it came in the garden in our backyard, others in the contented smile of my husband after a day of waltzing with words or our children's shouts of joy after discovering freshly laid eggs in the chicken coop. Pieces came in new friendships enjoyed over egg casserole or glasses of wine.

And the biggest portion so far has came in the form of this cross-country trip.

At one point, I questioned God's ability to give good gifts. I don't question it any longer. I don't ask why he took everything away because I now know that it wasn't everything, only a small pile of brick and metal that wasn't worth the price of my life.

And He gave me an adventure instead. Because the best gift giver doesn't give you a photo of a waterfall. No, He takes you to the foot of that waterfall, lets its billowy mists dampen your hair, the thunder of its lusty descent vibrate in your chest, and the coolness of its waters quench your thirst.

So this leg of our journey comes to an end, but I sit on the edge of my seat, forehead pressed against the window, eager for this adventure to continue.

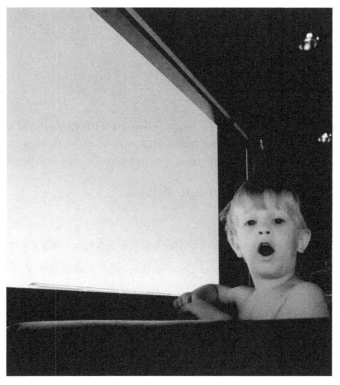

Sam sitting in his favorite spot, marveling at something he's just seen. Probably a volcano.

"Do not trouble your hearts overmuch with thought of the road tonight. Maybe the paths that you each shall tread are already laid before your feet, though you do not see them."

J.R.R. Tolkien

It's Thursday afternoon as I write this, and it's quiet and it's hot. A few flies buzz around the door where the sun reaches in and scorches the bus's black leather passenger seat. Maile and the kids fled to a small lakeside beach not far from where we are parked. Through the vents, I can hear the A/C rush and roar, but it cannot catch up.

The bus is messy, as it usually is at this time in the afternoon. An empty cereal box stands at leaning attention. A sippy cup, a styrofoam cup, a random shoe, a plastic deer, and a John Deere tractor clutter the floor under the table. The couch I'm sitting on holds a box of Legos, two of the kids' backpacks, Maile's purse, and a pile of homeschooling folders.

But soon, it will all be over. By Saturday night, we hope to have this bus parked in my parents' driveway, and by Monday, it will be cleaned out. We will probably never spend a night in it again. How strange.

Two weeks ago, we were parked in a beautiful campground in South Dakota, wearing sweaters and coats. One month ago, Salinas, California, and we hadn't yet lost our brakes. Five or six weeks ago, we were in windy Amarillo, a visit that seems to have taken place years in the past. Tulsa, New Orleans, Memphis, Nashville, Sarasota, Gainesville, Orlando, Charlotte, Bremo Bluff – all seem like settings in a book I read, long ago.

Four months ago (or one week before we left on our trip), I could not have begun to envision the amazing people we were about to meet in person, or the awesomeness of the landscape, or the heart-in-mouth moments of stress, anger, and fear. We've experienced things I never could have imagined.

This is an adventure: setting out to do something that doesn't make sense, something for which you are not completely equipped, something that takes you into a place fraught with danger or uncertainty. This is true of changing professions or moving or writing a book. It is true of saying hello to a stranger or giving away money for which you had a very good use. There are many ways to embark on an adventure, and very few of them involve a big blue bus named Willie.

Also, this about adventures: there are many terrible things that can happen along the way, and many terrible things that WILL happen along the way, but one of the worst things that could possibly happen is that you return unchanged.

We return from our adventure with very little to show for it – at least in a material sense. We have a good deal less money, not much work lined up, and for at least a few weeks, we will be living with our parents. Again. By most measures used by this world, taking this trip was a mistake, and it has left us worse off than when we began.

Thankfully, there are other means with which to measure a life. Ones less arbitrary than the numbers on a bank statement.

I know my wife better than I did before. I now understand why she wanted to take the trip, something I didn't know before we left. I have a better understanding of what she needs from me, and I understand (at least a little more) how I can provide her with that. I now see that she *does* put her right hand up over her chest while she reads something that moves her.

I've learned how much my children need me to be present for them. What a soft heart Cade has. Lucy's yearning for affection. Abra's enjoyment of a messy, crazy, moving life. How, when Sam watches the landscape go by, it tames his savage side. His "Red Rackham" side.

I've changed, too, but in less tangible ways, ways that I have trouble articulating. At least right now. Give me a few days. I'll let you know.

It has been quite an adventure. I wish you knew how much I appreciated the fact that you took the time to join us, to read our posts, to comment, to encourage. The countless emails that I received from people who were inspired by our trip, in turn, inspired us to keep going. We didn't always want to keep going. But we did.

So for now, I say good-bye from the road. The next time we meet, I'll be in my parent's basement again. Full circle. Looking for writing work. Going to visit grandma. Taking my aunt for her chemo treatments, if she'll have me. That's another thing I've learned on this trip: I can have little adventures every day, if I'll just get outside of myself.

In the words of J.R.R. Tolkien, who penned perhaps the greatest adventure story ever written:

Don't adventures ever have an end? I suppose not. Someone else always has to carry on the story.

So, carry on our story. Take an adventure. I can see it in your eyes.

You could use one.

We made it home (Shawn's dad made the sign).

If you enjoyed this book, consider purchasing Shawn's ebook,

Building a Life Out of Words.

It tells the story of the years leading up to this cross-country

trip

and how he and Maile lost their business and their house

and it was one of the best things that ever

could have happened to them.

Acknowledgments

This trip wouldn't have been possible without the kindness of so many people along the way, most of whom we never even met in person before we pulled out of the driveway. Thanks...

To Gerry for letting us park in your church parking lot on our first two nights. Apologies for running over your curbs.

To Shawna for the kid-perfect gifts (especially that eerie 21 Questions machine), and to Jake, for creating *Location, Location,* a CD that will always remind us of some of the best months of our lives.

To Dan and Tiffany, for letting us get the bus stuck in the ditch at the end of your driveway. Your house was a peaceful place for us to recover from that traumatic incident.

To Glen, for a delicious Harrisonburg pizza and a gym that gave our kids a much needed place to run around. Thanks, man.

To Andi, Woody and Caruso, for welcoming us on to a farm that now feels like home, for the smores and the history lesson, for the tractor rides and the trailer pin, for the water hose and the delicious meal. And of course, for your wonderful friendship.

To Maile's parents, and to Matthew and Suzanne, for helping us find a place to park Willie for a week, and for always supporting us even in our zaniest endeavors.

To Tamara, for what we will forever remember as The Long Walk. Thanks for taking time out of your busy life to show us around Gainesville and be our friend on the road.

One of Shawn's favorite nights of the trip took place at a little wine bar in Orlando. Thanks, Stacy, for sharing your evening and your friends with us.

To Renault, for letting us park Willie in the sandy lot beside your church.

To Eric, Julie and Leslie, for spending an afternoon with Shawn and sharing all your writing secrets. We're looking forward to our next visit to Sarasota so that we can do it again.

To Katie Troyer, for being a great neighbor in Sarasota.

To Jeff and Katie, for all the wonderful things you are doing in Atlanta. Your generosity and love for those in your neighborhood is amazing. Thanks for dinner, and for lending your back yard to our kids.

To MPT, for a friendship that has literally taken me around the world. Thanks for having coffee with me in Nashville, dinner in Dubai, breakfast in Colombo, and for your unwavering support. You are awesome.

To Bryan, for inviting Maile and I to Killer Tribes conference and for inspiring me to build community...and also for all of the breakfast pep talks at Four Sisters.

To everyone at Killer Tribes, but especially the wonderful groups we had lunch and dinner with. You know who you are.

To Sharideth, for buying us dinner in Nashville and treating us like visiting VIPs.

To Ryan and Kim, for allowing us to mark up your front yard with very wide bus tire tracks, letting us help you start your garden, letting Shawn mow your yard, and letting our children run amock throughout your house. We love you guys.

To Ron and Nancy, for putting us up in that hotel suite and nearly bringing Maile to tears (of relief). Thanks for giving the kids golf cart rides around the warehouse, cooking up that delicious barbeque, and generally being such amazing hosts – we were sorry to leave Memphis.

To the Lady at the seafood market in New Orleans, for teaching us how to "bole" a crab and decapitate a shrimp. ("Bole" translates to "boil," for all of you Northerners.)

To all those Mosquitoes in New Orleans, for nothing.

To Uncle Chub, for a level of generosity that left us astounded. You were one of our most loyal supporters, and your constant texts of encouragement always left us with smiles on our faces (or tears in our eyes). Thanks for playing hide and seek with us, buying breakfast, driving all the way to San Antonio when you couldn't wait to see us, and showing us Austin. Our kids will always remember that city because of you.

To Lore: who knew we would discover such a kindred spirit in the middle of a country-sized state? Our night of thoughtful conversation with you was one of the trip's highlights.

To the McVickers, for being friends to us wherever we are! What a fun night! What a delicious meal! What a wonderful friendship! Thank you.

To the Luitwielers, for a much-needed taste of normal life. Thanks for the incredible chicken, the fun soccer games, the coffee-shop writers' gathering, and for introducing us to Tulsa. We almost ended our trip there and put down roots. Our loss for not doing it.

To Jason and Aimee, for welcoming us into your home and letting our children terrorize your dog. Jason, I enjoyed hearing your take on writing and meeting the community of creative folks in your area. Amarillo was one of the highlights of our trip.

To Sharon and the rest of the folks at the Buffalo Bookstore in Canyon, for the best gift basket I've ever received.

After four straight days of rain and clouds, we will never believe you, Aunt Kate, when you say that Pasadena is "never this way." Seeing your face just after the halfway point of our trip was a huge ray of sunshine. We're so happy you gave in and moved East.

To Heather, for hosting a wonderful writers' gathering at your beautiful home.

To the Mountains of California, for being breath-taking.

To the Sierra-Nevada Mountains and the rest stop commemorating the Donner Party, for being kind of creepy.

To the Teton Pass, for changing our lives. Seriously.

To Chris and Julie, for allowing us to be present at the first church service in your new facility. What an incredible story. Thanks for letting our bus leak oil all over your old parking lot, thanks for feeding us, and thanks for giving us a little place of peace for a few days.

In just a few short hours, we fell in love with a family only halfway to Normal. Jason, Kristin and girls, thanks for a wonderful evening, a dizzying playground, and some delicious food. It was fun talking creativity with you guys.

To Glen and Mary Jane, we couldn't have done this trip without you. Thanks for sharing your life with us and putting us up in the best campground in Indiana.

To Joy and Scott, for cheering us on during the entire trip. We were so disappointed to cruise through your part of the world at two in the morning. Next time the Bennett-Smucker craziness will commence.

To Shawn's parents, for letting us move back into the basement (again) and for being some of our most enthusiastic cheerleaders.

To all of the bloggers, authors, creative folks, friends and enemies who have helped to spread the news about this book's release. We appreciate you so much.

Most of all, MOST OF ALL, to Sam and Melody, for your irrational willingness to trust us with your bus, for a wild sort of reckless generosity that has changed our lives, for always always

always supporting our unorthodox lifestyle, for the generous gift you gave us the night before we pulled away from my parents' house, and for basically being the kind of people that we hope to be to our own nephews and nieces someday. We wish we could tell everyone everything that you've done for us, but we also know that if we did that, Sam would wring our necks, so for now we simply say, Thank You.

Made in the USA
Las Vegas, NV
16 July 2023

74814116R00148